FINDING YOUR VOICE

FINDING YOUR VOICE

A Comprehensive Guide to Collegiate Policy Debate

Allison Hahn
Taylor Ward Hahn
Marie-Odile N. Hobeika

International Debate Education Association
New York, London & Amsterdam

Published by:
International Debate Education Association
105 East 22nd Street
New York, NY 10010

Copyright © 2013 by Allison Hahn, Taylor Ward Hahn, and Marie-Odile N. Hobeika
This work is licensed under the Creative Commons Attribution License:
http://creativecommons.org/licenses/by-nc-nd/3.0/

Library of Congress Cataloging-in-Publication Data

Hahn, Allison.
  Finding your voice : a comprehensive guide to collegiate policy debate / Allison Hahn, Taylor Ward Hahn, Marie-Odile N. Hobeika.
      pages cm
   ISBN 978-1-61770-051-4
   1. Debates and debating. I. Hahn, Taylor Ward. II. Hobeika, Marie-Odile N. III. Title.
   PN4181.H24 2013
   808.53--dc23
                              2012042433

Design by Kathleen Hayes
Printed in the USA

CONTENTS

Preface vii

Chapter 1: Basics of Policy Debate 1

Chapter 2: The Policy Debate Squad 11

Chapter 3: The Topic Process 16

Chapter 4: Arguments 22

Chapter 5: Evidence 35

Chapter 6: Responsibilities of the Affirmative and Negative 59

Chapter 7: Speaking and Flowing 67

Chapter 8: Speeches 76

Chapter 9: Cross-Examination 97

Chapter 10: The 1AC 112

Chapter 11: The Negative Strategy 136

Chapter 12: Stock Issues 144

Chapter 13: Topicality 153

Chapter 14: Disadvantages 170

Chapter 15: Counterplans 186

Chapter 16: Kritiks 201

Chapter 17: Judging the Debate 220

Chapter 18: Your First Tournament 230

Chapter 19: "Oh Shit" List 237

Appendixes 255
Appendix A: Speaking Drills 255
Appendix B: Cross-Examination Cheat Sheet Guide 259
Appendix C: List of Abbreviations 262
Appendix D: Paperless Debate 265
Appendix E: Resources 269

Glossary 272

PREFACE

The text that you hold in your hands was created through the combined efforts of three debate coaches who needed a guide for their novice debaters. Having taught at universities and high schools across the United States, we began to notice a trend in the debate community: novices often lacked the information necessary to quickly learn how to compete in policy debate. Exchanging ideas, we each discovered that teaching someone the basics of policy debate was often a haphazard exercise for debater and coach alike. Our own experience was that we had spent years providing preparatory lectures, activities, practice debates—but at the end of the day, our students asked, "what can I read to be ready for tomorrow?" So we searched for a comprehensive guide to policy debate and found several. Some books were written as textbooks, but we were not teaching a course. Other books were aimed exclusively at high school students, and, while interesting, they did not address the complexity of our students' questions. The last set of books had excellent coverage of standard policy debate arguments but had not kept up with the newest argument strategies. Failing to find an appropriate text, we came together to create a series of crash-course guides to policy debate—those guides were the building blocks for this book. We hope that this text will make beginning to debate a bit easier and lead you to one of the most enjoyable activities available to students.

Debaters are smart and ambitious learners, so any worthwhile introduction to policy debate must be both stimulating and educationally varied. Some debaters begin with a preference for specific argument styles; others want to sample a variety of argument styles before determining their own style or strategy. Occasionally, a novice debater begins her career by debating with a varsity debater and needs a quick introduction to everything that could happen during the round.

To meet your needs, and the various needs of each of our readers, the chapters in this book are self-contained. You can read from cover to cover, gradually building your knowledge of debate skills and arguments. Or, if it is the night before your first tournament and you are unclear about a particular issue, you can delve into one specific topic. The most useful information, however, might be found near the end of the text where we have included cheat sheets and an "Oh Shit" list for a number of problems that you might encounter.

Our combined experiences in debate have given us a pretty comprehensive and diverse knowledge base. Each of us debated in high school and college, traveling across the country as debaters and later as coaches. Two of us embrace Kritiks, the third prefers policy arguments. We have debated in front of the most radical and most conservative judges in the country and have tried to prepare you for both extremes. Yet, even as we prepare you to succeed in a debate tournament, try to remember that this community is not only about competition. Policy debate is a cornucopia of ideas, allowing students to explore concepts and ideas together in pursuit of their personal and intellectual goals. Debate alumni include John F. Kennedy, Oprah Winfrey, Jimmy Carter, Hillary Clinton, Malcolm X, and Gen. David Petraeus. These individuals have all made their mark on history not because they won or lost a round of debate, but because they learned to think quickly and clearly, explain their opinions concisely, and find evidence to support their ideas.

Being a policy debater will teach you how to argue, and, even more important, you will learn to ask sophisticated questions, open yourself to new ideas, and gain in-depth knowledge of a wide range of topics. You will hone your presentation skills and become more confident in presenting your opinion, even if it contradicts that of everyone else in the room. This book only lays out the tools for participating in policy debate; we hope that it will accompany, not replace, your experience of competing at tournaments and entering the policy debate community.

A debate community is only as vibrant as the people who gather to grow from one another's arguments. To paraphrase a great coach, Ross K. Smith: Thank you, our coaches, debaters, and teammates, who have pushed us to think harder, research deeper, get outside of our narrower confines. You pose questions without which we could not learn and improve. We couldn't do it without you.

1

BASICS OF POLICY DEBATE

This chapter introduces the basics of policy debate, including people, format, resolution, arguments, judges, and skills. We will investigate each of these topics in more detail in later chapters.

What Is Policy Debate?

Policy debate is an educational competition in which participants debate the merit(s) of adopting a specific policy designed to address and remedy a contemporary problem. Policy options proposed during the debate must fall under the annual pre-arranged topic called "the resolution." Debate squads begin preparing research and arguments specific to the resolution during the summer. Competition begins in the fall at weekend tournaments. Each debate involves four debaters organized into two teams who are evaluated by a judge. The Affirmative team proposes a policy and the Negative team is expected to refute whatever policy the Affirmative presents. All teams are required to argue on both Affirmative and Negative sides throughout the course of a debate tournament.

People

The collegiate policy debate community consists of competitors and coaches affiliated with American colleges and universities. Debate programs are referred to as "squads" and vary in size and structure according to the financial resources and priorities of the institution. Although all policy debate squads are affiliated with a college or university, the nature of the affiliation varies among schools. Some teams have well-funded, university-sponsored programs with entire buildings dedicated to their use. Others are student-run clubs that receive small grants from their colleges to pay for a few tournaments each semester.

Some squads are directed by a professional head coach who manages all administrative and coaching details; some by a group of volunteers or students; and some by a coaching staff of professor-directors, graduate student coaches, and paid assistants. These individuals are in charge of making all travel arrangements, planning meetings, and coaching individual teams. At tournaments, your coaches will serve as judges—though you will never be judged by your own coach. Each debate round will have at least one judge who is responsible for deciding the winning team.

The policy debate format calls for two-person teams. Generally, novices pair with other novices, though occasionally a novice might be teamed with a more experienced debater. Many debaters try out different partners until they find a partner who complements their strengths, weaknesses, and personality.

Format

Policy debate follows a standard format for speaking order and speech length during the debate round. Each round involves two teams of two debaters (a total of four debaters). The Affirmative team supports a plan of action (the plan) pertaining to a predetermined policy proposal called "the resolution." This plan must meet each of the five "stock issues" that clarify the key aspects of the plan: inherency (has the plan been already done); harms (why is the plan necessary); topicality (does the plan apply to the resolution); solvency (will the plan work); and significance (how large is the plan). The Negative can oppose the Affirmative's proposed policy action directly, prove that the Affirmative has not met one of the stock issues, or attack the merits of the resolution in general.

Each Affirmative and Negative debater gives one constructive speech and one rebuttal speech. A constructive speech is used to outline the team's arguments. Because these speeches present new arguments, each constructive speech is followed by three minutes of cross-examination. The rebuttal speech is used to refute the opponent's arguments, build on the debater's own critical arguments, and explain to the judge why your team has won the round. New arguments should not be presented in the rebuttals.

Speech Times in the Round

1st Affirmative Constructive (1AC)	9 minutes
Cross-Examination of 1AC by 2nd Negative Speaker	3 minutes

1st Negative Constructive (1NC)	9 minutes
Cross-Examination of 1NC by 1AC	3 minutes
2nd Affirmative Constructive (2AC)	9 minutes
Cross-Examination of 2AC by 1NC	3 minutes
2nd Negative Construction (2NC)	9 minutes
Cross-Examination of 2NC by 2AC	3 minutes
1st Negative Rebuttal (1NR)	6 minutes
1st Affirmative Rebuttal (1AR)	6 minutes
2nd Negative Rebuttal (2NR)	6 minutes
2nd Affirmative Rebuttal (2AR)	6 minutes

Typically, the debater who gives the first constructive also gives the first rebuttal. Thus, the debater who presents the 1AC also presents the 1AR, and the debater who presents the 2NC also presents the 2NR.

Tournaments have six-to-eight preliminary rounds and a series of elimination rounds. Policy debate facilitates "switch-side" debating—in half the rounds of a tournament you will be Affirmative; for the other half, you will be Negative. Sometimes switch-side debate makes you feel like you are debating against your own arguments. Advocating a policy in one round and then arguing against it in the next can be difficult. Nevertheless, switch-side debating follows a tradition, begun in ancient Greece, of examining both sides of an issue before determining which to support.

Resolution

The resolution is a carefully crafted proposition that allows debaters to focus on the debate topic for the entire school year. A fairly designed resolution covers a rich field of research that allows both Affirmative and Negative teams to create arguments. Debaters refer to this field of research as "ground" and believe that a "fair division of ground" exists when expert scholars and policymakers have published a wealth of literature that supports both sides of the resolution. Using one resolution per year enables the teams to do in-depth research and conduct extensive investigations into the subject.

The process of developing the annual resolution begins each summer, when the debate community first votes on a general topic area, for example, education or nuclear weapons policy. From this topic area, the debate community creates several carefully worded resolutions and then votes on one for the next year of debate. For example, the 2010–2011 topic area was immigration and the resolution was:

> Resolved: The United States Federal Government should substantially increase the number of and/or substantially expand beneficiary eligibility for its visas for one or more of the following: employment-based immigrant visas, nonimmigrant temporary worker visas, family-based visas, human trafficking–based visas.

This was considered to be a fair resolution because literature exists for both the Affirmative (increase visas) and Negative (do not increase visas) sides of the resolution.

Arguments for the Affirmative

During a debate, the Affirmative's goal is to prove that the resolution is both a good idea and better than the status quo (Latin for "the existing state of affairs"). The collection of arguments supporting a change in the status quo is called the "Affirmative case." The Affirmative case must prove all of the stock issues—inherency, harms, topicality, solvency, and significance—if pressed by the Negative. Each team can choose how to organize their Affirmative case, but most teams prefer to use the following sections: inherency, harms or advantages, the plan, solvency, and significance because this organization creates a better narrative flow. All Affirmatives will include the stock issues but may not list them explicitly unless challenged by the Negative. Affirmative teams can choose whether to include a section of their case titled either "harms" or "advantages" depending on how these arguments are being presented. Harms are organized to prove that the Affirmative addresses and remedies ongoing deleterious issues in the status quo. Advantages prove that the Affirmative either causes something good to happen or prevents a future problem from developing.

Let's use the resolution "Resolved: The United States Federal Government should increase funding for employment and training initiatives for the homeless in the United States," to see how each section supports the Affirmative case.

> **Inherency** describes the status quo in the topic area. In this case the Affirmative might maintain that "Government and nonprofit commitments to help the homeless are decreasing."
>
> **Harms** describe what conditions have developed in the status quo as a result of inherency. For example, "Homelessness is increasing in America."

Advantages explain potential benefits of carrying out the plan. For example, "The plan increases employment. This helps the economy and raises the standard of living for all Americans."

The plan presents an action that falls within the parameters of the resolution and solves the harms. For example, "The United States Federal Government should increase funding for the Homeless Veterans Reintegration Program."

Solvency explains how the plan will work. For example, "The Homeless Veterans Reintegration Program solves homelessness by creating long-term self-reliance for military personnel facing economic hardship."

Arguments for the Negative

The Negative must prove that the risks associated with the Affirmative's plan outweigh the potential benefits. They do this by presenting a number of different types of arguments. Arguments that specifically attack the Affirmative's inherency, harms, advantages, or solvency are referred to as "on-case" arguments. Arguments that attack the Affirmative by detailing unanticipated side effects or presenting theoretical objections to the plan are called "off-case" arguments. The four most common off-case arguments are the stock issue of topicality, and disadvantages, counterplans, and Kritiks.

Topicality argues that the Affirmative should lose because they are trying to solve a problem that is not included in the resolution, making the plan not "topical." In debate jargon, we call this being "off topic."

Disadvantages, known as disads or DAs, argue that the Affirmative's plan will lead to political or economic problems.

Counterplans, known as CPs, argue that while action is warranted, the Affirmative has chosen the wrong course of action.

Kritiks (German for "critique") argue that the Affirmative's plan is flawed on a conceptual level.

Judging Arguments

Judges take detailed notes on both teams' arguments during the debate round. Based on the arguments, the judge will determine a winner of the round. The most common methods that judges use to evaluate the round are "policymaking" and "tabula rasa" (Latin for "clean slate"). Judges who use a policymaking method have the perspective that they are legislators voting on a policy. They determine the winner of a debate based on whether or not they have been convinced that the Affirmative's plan should be adopted by the United States Federal Government. Tabula rasa judges allow debaters to assign them a role in the round, whether it be as a social activist or a civic educator. These judges claim to have no preconceived biases about how the debate should occur and no preconceived way of viewing arguments. Tabula rasa judges are willing to evaluate arguments based on the paradigm or standards that the debaters propose. Other judging philosophies exist, but the most important responsibility of any judge is to evaluate only the arguments in the round and not allow personal convictions to sway her evaluation.

Skills

Policy debate emphasizes public speaking skills, quick and accurate speech, analytical capabilities, and research skills. While all of these are important for collegiate policy debate, coaches place varying emphasis on different skills. For example, some coaches specialize in training debaters to speak extremely quickly in order to make more arguments. Other coaches want their debaters to speak slowly, making fewer arguments but demonstrating excellent presentation skills. Some debaters conduct all of their own research, while others debate for a squad that has a staff of researchers who find the most up-to-date arguments.

Most squads are varied, with some members focusing on only one skill and other debaters developing proficiency in multiple areas. Both approaches have advantages. Debaters who focus only on one skill become exceptionally proficient in that area. Debaters who aim toward proficiency in multiple areas gain a range of knowledge, but are perhaps not as deeply educated in one area. As a community, we embrace this variety; it is part of what makes debate interesting.

KEY CONCEPTS

1. Policy debate squads consist of debaters and coaches and are affiliated with a college or university.

2. During a policy debate, two teams of two individuals debate the merits of the resolution in a series of constructive and rebuttal speeches, with one team supporting and other opposing the resolution.

3. All debate rounds follow the same order of speeches, requiring each debater to present one constructive (9 minute) and one rebuttal (6 minute) speech.

4. Each team must be prepared to debate both the Affirmative and the Negative sides of the resolution during every tournament.

5. The Affirmative team supports the resolution by presenting a case that proves why acting as directed by the resolution is superior to the status quo.

6. If pressed by the Negative, the Affirmative must prove that they satisfy the five stock issues: inherency, harms, topicality, solvency, and significance.

7. The Affirmative case has five parts: inherency, harms, plan, advantages, and solvency.

8. The Negative opposes the Affirmative case by presenting on-case and off-case arguments.

9. A judge determines the winner of the debate round by using one of two judging philosophies: policymaking or tabula rasa.

2

THE POLICY DEBATE SQUAD

Policy debate squads can operate like a well-oiled machine, a tight-knit family, or a social club. Although each team's dynamic is distinct, the community has basic standards for who belongs to a debate squad and how those members interact. This chapter introduces the members of the squad—the head coach, assistant coach(es), debaters, and debate partners. It also addresses the structure of the debate squad, focusing on members' responsibilities, what makes a good debate partnership, and how that partnership is formed.

The Head Coach

Most debate squads are run by a head coach, usually a tenured professor who participated in policy debate as a student and now directs both the administrative and educational elements of the squad. In most squads, the head coach is responsible for the budget and makes the final decisions about partner pairings, tournament travel schedules, and the requirements for team membership. The head coach is also responsible for teaching the squad research, critical thinking, and speaking skills.

A student's relationship with the head coach should be amicable yet professional. Some head coaches happily serve as life coaches, helping students balance their academic and personal lives. However, unless you are given explicit permission, avoid calling the head coach late at night with personal problems and do not camp out in her office.

Some squads have only one coach. When this is the case, the head coach will travel to all tournaments and serve as the go-to authority for all questions about argument development. On larger squads, the head coach has a team of assistant coaches who divide this work and give personal coaching to individual squad members.

The Assistant Coach

Assistant coaches are extremely knowledgeable about debate but have less academic experience and have usually debated more recently than the head coach. These coaches are in charge of fine-tuning debaters' skills and carrying out goals set by the head coach. While it is the job of debaters to conduct most of their own research, some assistant coaches will stay up all night researching answers to the latest arguments. Others will travel to tournaments and provide pre-round coaching.

When should a debater approach an assistant coach for help? The short answer is: as soon as you need it. If you're having problems with another squad member or don't understand an argument, discussing the issue with an assistant coach is the best option. Of course, keep in mind that many assistant coaches are also graduate students with teaching assignments. Until you know the assistant coach well, make formal appointments so that you can work at a time convenient for both of you.

The Squad

The debate squad consists of all debaters and coaches who cooperate for research, training, practice, and competition. Debaters in the squad come with varied experience. Some debaters will join the squad as freshmen, but with four years of policy debate experience from high school. Others will join having no previous debate experience or having participated in other forms of debate. Since everyone joins a squad with a different debate background and goal, collegiate policy debate is divided into three divisions: novice, JV (junior varsity), and varsity (or open division). Coaches will help teams determine what division is appropriate for them based on division eligibility, experience, and the skills of the debaters.

Some squads hold weekly meetings, others operate in smaller research groups and only hold squad meetings before tournaments. Usually these meetings are held in the squad room, an office at the university that functions as both a work area and a place for team members to socialize.

Not all squad members will approach debate in the same way. Some debaters attend only one tournament a semester, while others compete every week. Some debaters sacrifice their grades for debate wins; others will not even think about debate until all of their schoolwork is complete. Take time to find your own style, but always remember that debate is an extracurricular activity. It should be fun, engaging, and educational.

Your Debate Partner

Policy debaters compete in pairs; partners spend a considerable amount of time working together. Some debate partners become best friends; other debaters have several partners in one debate season. On some teams, the coach or assistant coach will assign partners and then make changes as necessary. On other teams, students choose their partners without coaching assistance. No matter how partnerships are formed, remember that partners do not have to share academic years or majors. Ideal partners tend to have complementary rather than identical skills, so don't be surprised if at first glance a set of partners has little in common. The most important factors for any successful partnership are comparable debate goals, compatible personalities, and work schedules that mesh well.

KEY CONCEPTS

1. The head coach is usually a tenured faculty member with experience in debate who sees to all of the team's administrative and educational requirements.

2. Assistant coaches are graduate students assigned to give individual coaching advice, supervise research assignments, and travel to tournaments.

3. The debate squad consists of all debaters and coaches from a university who cooperate for research, training, practice, and travel.

4. Debate partnerships are arranged between two debaters from the squad, usually in consultation with a coach or assistant coach.

5. A strong debate partnership is grounded in comparable debate goals, compatible personalities, and work schedules that mesh well.

3

THE TOPIC PROCESS

The policy debate topic and subsequent resolution are chosen annually through a democratic process. This chapter will explain what a debate topic is, how it is chosen, and how the topic is used to formulate a resolution that can spur and support a year's worth of educational debate. While novice debaters do not usually propose new resolutions, understanding why you are debating a specific topic will make debate more enjoyable and educational.

Choosing the Topic

Policy debaters often use the terms "topic" and "resolution" interchangeably, but each word relates to a different part of the larger process of determining the yearly debate resolution. The debate topic is a broad issue such as immigration, nuclear weapons policy, or agricultural subsidies. The debate resolution is a declaratory statement advocating a specific policy initiative within the topic area. The resolution is what is debated during tournament rounds.

The procedure for developing a vague idea into an official debate resolution is known as the "topic process." All stages of the topic process are administered by the topic committee of the Cross Examination Debate Association, one of the primary policy debate organizations that govern the rules and norms of policy debate. This organization facilitates discussion of the topic and oversees the voting that determines the year's resolution.

Every topic begins with an idea. Somewhere in the debate community, someone is already thinking of a debate topic that could evolve into next year's resolution. One of the wonderful aspects of the topic process is that coaches and administrators do not control it—any debater can propose a topic.

The first stage of the topic process is the submission of a topic paper that argues that the proposed topic could facilitate a year of debate. The Cross Examination Debate Association publishes electronic copies of the topic papers at the beginning of the summer. Debate squads then read and discuss the topic papers and submit a ballot that ranks their preferences. Finally, the topic committee tabulates the results and, through a series of elimination rounds, one topic is chosen.

Developing the Resolution

Once a general topic area is selected, community members begin a new round of proposals to determine how the resolution will be worded. These "wording papers" focus on the specific nuances of the topic literature and work to construct a resolution that will provide a fair division of arguments (fair ground) for both the Affirmative and Negative.

The wording of potential resolutions is discussed at a series of meetings that are chaired by prominent debate coaches and directors. These meetings are open to all debate participants by either physically attending or participating in streaming discussions over the Internet. Debaters are encouraged to attend or stream the meetings since participating in the topic process is a great way to learn about the subtle nuances of the coming year's resolution. At the meeting's conclusion, the committee distributes a list of resolution wording options for a final round of voting. As before, each squad receives one ballot to electronically rank each of the resolution options.

The Debate Resolution

Although the topic of the resolution differs from year to year, all resolutions include an actor and at least one broad policy option. Here are some examples of previous resolutions:

(2010–2011) Resolved: The United States Federal Government should substantially increase the number of and/or substantially expand beneficiary eligibility for its visas for one or more of the following: employment-based immigrant visas, nonimmigrant temporary worker visas, family-based visas, human trafficking-based visas.

(2009–2010) Resolved: The United States Federal Government should substantially reduce the size of its nuclear weapons arsenal, and/or substantially reduce and restrict the role and/or missions of its nuclear weapons arsenal.

(2006–2007) Resolved: The United States Supreme Court should overrule one or more of the following decisions: *Planned Parenthood v. Casey*, 505 U.S. 833 (1992); *Ex parte*

Quirin, 317 U.S. 1 (1942); *U.S. v. Morrison*, 529 U.S. 598 (2000); *Milliken v. Bradley*, 418 U.S. 717 (1974).

(2002–2003) Resolved: The United States Federal Government should ratify or accede to, and implement, one or more of the following:

- The Comprehensive Nuclear Test Ban Treaty;
- The Kyoto Protocol;
- The Rome Statute of the International Criminal Court;
- The Second Optional Protocol to the International Covenant on Civil and Political Rights aiming at the abolition of the death penalty;
- The treaty between the United States of America and the Russian Federation on Strategic Offensive Reductions, if not ratified by the United States.

(2000–2001) Resolved: That the United States Federal Government should substantially increase its development assistance, including increasing government-to-government assistance, within the Greater Horn of Africa.

Each resolution calls for the United States Federal Government (the actor) to take direct action on a specific issue. However, the type, specificity, and agent of action changes every year. Some resolutions, such as the 2002–2003 resolution, call for the government to take action on one or more items in a narrow, bulleted list. This type of resolution is commonly referred to as a "list resolution" and is preferred by some debaters because it dramatically limits the scope of the resolution. Other resolutions, such as the nuclear weapons resolution from 2009–2010, are broader in scope and call for an action in a given area of domestic policy. Some debaters prefer these broader resolutions because they allow more freedom to interpret what action the federal government should take. While most resolutions have a generic federal actor (United States Federal Government), some specify the branch of government. For example, the 2006–2007 resolution called for the United States Supreme Court to overturn one or more of its rulings.

Deciding how to word a resolution is a difficult but critical process. If a resolution is worded poorly, it will create an unequal distribution of ground between the Affirmative and Negative, thus making a fair debate impossible. To illustrate the importance of wording a resolution, consider the following: "Resolved: That the Commander-in-Chief power of the President of the United States should be substantially curtailed." This resolution, debated in the 1993–1994 academic year, was considered successful because it provided a fair distribution of ground to both sides. The Affirmative was charged with decreasing the powers of the president and the Negative could argue that current or increased powers were preferable. If the resolution had been worded: "Resolved: That the Commander-in-Chief power of the President of the United States should be substantially *changed*," the resolution would have been less fair. The second wording would not maintain an even division of ground because Affirmatives could propose virtually any policy change involving presidential powers—both increasing and decreasing commander-in-chief powers would be topical. Negative teams would have no way of predicting how the Affirmative would act or how large their action would be. Consequently, Negative teams could not adequately prepare for the round and the Affirmative would win a disproportionate number of debates.

Paying attention to how individual words and phrases alter the debate resolution is not easy, but doing so provides the necessary foundation to understand and use texts in the debate round. Dedicating significant time to learning the wording and context of the resolution at the beginning of the debate season will make the rest of the year far more educational and competitively successful.

KEY CONCEPTS

1. The topic is an overarching idea from which the debate resolution is formed.

2. The resolution delineates a precisely worded issue based on the topic.

3. The resolution is selected through a democratic process. Any member of the debate community can propose a resolution. During the voting process, each debate squad receives one vote.

4. Resolutions are selected based on their importance for society and "fair division of ground," or the availability of research, that allows teams to both support and oppose the resolution.

5. Resolutions are designed to address contemporary issues. Each word in the resolution is carefully considered to ensure the fairest possible division between Affirmative and Negative arguments.

4

ARGUMENTS

Policy debate requires each team to present a complex set of arguments in a short time. To regulate, process, and respond to these arguments, debaters have adopted a common organizational pattern. This chapter begins with the basics of an argument: a claim and a warrant. After explaining the fundamentals of a claim and the two types of warrants (analytic and evidentiary), this chapter presents the three types of arguments found in policy debate: theory, policy, and Kritik.

Claims and Warrants

All debate arguments follow the same structure of presenting a claim and a warrant. The claim is a one-sentence assertive statement of what the debater will prove. For example, "guns save lives."

By itself, this claim is meaningless; your opponent and the judge have no way of determining what kind of guns save lives, how they save lives, where these lives are saved, or even why those lives were at risk. A claim is incomplete without its corresponding warrant—the reason why the claim should be accepted. This part of the argument is presented either by using your own arguments (referred to as "analytical warrants") or by quoting published academic or government analysis (referred to as "evidence"). Using the guns example, the claim "guns save lives" could be supported by the analytical warrant "because criminals will be deterred by the expectation that their intended victim is carrying a gun" or by evidence from a qualified source, such as government report, that provides statistics showing that areas with more guns have fewer gun-related deaths.

Why We Use This Structure

Organizing arguments into claims and warrants can seem unnatural or repetitive to the novice debater. However, it is at the novice level that this standard of argument construction is most helpful. Using this structure teaches novices to quickly deliver information and efficiently make comparisons during a debate round. Additionally, because all debaters use the same structure, the judge is able to focus on comparing arguments rather than attempting to determine if claims were supported by warrants. Finally, using this structure allows debaters and judges to subdivide claims and warrants by type and determine the quality of their arguments. This subdivision becomes increasingly important during JV or varsity rounds, where the number of arguments delivered increases rapidly, making efficient delivery essential for both the speaker and judge.

Types of Claims

We can classify claims into three categories: warrantless, basic, and comparative. Understanding the difference among categories is essential both for attacking your opponent's arguments and understanding a judge's decision.

WARRANTLESS CLAIMS

Warrantless claims are underdeveloped arguments that contain an assertive statement, such as "peace is better than war," but do not provide a reason to support or explain the statement. These are bare bones arguments that do little to support your side in the round and will not win a debate. Sometimes debaters accidently make warrantless claims if they are running out of time or if they become confused. One or two warrantless claims won't hurt, but debaters should attempt to avoid them because they are easily defeated and eat up time better served by presenting basic or comparative claims.

BASIC CLAIMS

A basic claim is a clear, concise statement that summarizes the argument and is supported by a warrant. When presenting these statements, debaters should avoid rhetorical flourishes or esoteric verbs and use a basic subject, verb, object construction; for example, "Gun ownership deters crime." Basic claims are used at the beginning of a debate. While they will not win a debate round, they provide a foundation that later speeches can build on to make comparative claims.

COMPARATIVE CLAIMS

You can use a comparative claim both to attack your opponent and establish your own team's argument. For example, "despite the Affirmative's claims, gun ownership deters crime" is a comparative claim with two parts: 1) the Affirmative is wrong and 2) gun ownership deters crime. This type of claim can be made in any speech after the 1AC. While comparative claims take longer to explain, they are more powerful arguments than basic claims because they draw the judge's attention to how arguments clash. In policy debate, argument clash indicates a point of conflict between the arguments of the Affirmative and the Negative. Strong debaters will highlight points of clash and make comparative claims explaining why their side has won the argument.

Types of Warrants

Debaters support their claims by utilizing two types of warrants: analytical and evidentiary.

ANALYTICAL WARRANTS

Analytical warrants are created by the speaker. The debater begins with a claim such as "democracy prevents war" and then backs up this claim with her own thoughts and logic. For example, she might say "democracy prevents war because when all citizens have an opportunity to vote, they are less likely to take up arms to express their political opinions." She could support this argument with evidence, but she might choose not to because she can use an analytical warrant to craft her argument to specifically respond to her opponent's argument. Do not underestimate the strategic utility of analytical warrants. When well explained, analytical warrants are just as likely to win a debate as evidentiary warrants.

EVIDENTIARY WARRANTS

Quotations from journals, newspapers, books, reports, and government documents are all referred to as "evidence." Using evidence based on citations from experts or scholars is an excellent means of proving the validity of claims. However, they require research and preparation before the debate tournament and can take much longer to present in the round than analytical claims.

Unlike claims, no type of warrant is better than another. Each has its own place in debate, and the utility of a warrant varies depending on the particular argument, circumstances, and stylistic approach of the speaker. The balance between the analytical and evidentiary warrants also differs between constructive and rebuttal speeches. A strong debater will ensure that the constructive speech primarily contains evidentiary warrants and the rebuttal speech primarily contains analytical warrants. Many new debaters depend too greatly on evidentiary warrants, wrongfully assuming that the experts who wrote the evidence are more qualified than they are to speak in the debate round. Experienced debaters have learned to use evidentiary warrants as a means of strengthening their analytical arguments. Thus, they use their own words to frame the opinions and facts presented in pieces of evidence.

Types of Arguments

Policy debaters use three types of arguments: theory, policy, and Kritik. Strong debaters will include at least two of these in their constructive speeches. This variety provides debaters with a number of options for winning the round. Although the source and amount of research required for each type of argument differs, each argument type uses the same claim and warrant structure.

THEORY ARGUMENTS

Theory arguments are of two common types: action-specific and resolution-specific. Action-specific arguments assert that a team has violated a community norm, e.g., using too much speaking time or employing an unfair strategy. These arguments are based on the personal actions of the debaters and can also include assertions that the type and manner of arguments made by a team are unfair—presenting contradictory arguments or refusing to clarify their position until later in the debate, for instance. Resolution-specific arguments deal exclusively with asking if and how the Affirmative team has addressed the annual resolution correctly.

The most common type of resolution-specific theory argument is topicality. This argument claims that the Affirmative has "violated topicality" either because the plan is not a valid response to the resolution or because the Affirmative has made arguments outside of the scope of the year's resolution. Theory arguments usually begin with a claim and are supported by analytical warrants. For example:

> *Claim*: The Affirmative should lose because they violated topicality.
>
> *Analytical Warrant*: The debate community agreed on the topic "The United States Federal Government should ban guns," but the Affirmative is only proposing a way to limit gun ownership, not a way to ban guns. This is a debate for which we could not be expected to prepare. Therefore, this round is unfair, and voting against the Affirmative will force them to begin debating the topic.

POLICY ARGUMENTS

Policy arguments address the pragmatic desirability of the Affirmative plan—most often addressing economic and political considerations. These arguments are based on claims and warrants made by policymakers, analysts, think tanks, or the media. Policy arguments are almost always supported by evidence. A basic policy argument for the Affirmative on banning guns would be:

> *Claim*: The United States Federal Government should ban guns.
>
> *Evidentiary Warrant*: The U.S. Department of Health and Human Services reported in 2009 that nations that allow citizens to carry guns have a higher rate of crime, and high rates of crime deter economic and technical innovation.

This example highlights the relationship between the claim and the warrant. The claim is specifically tailored to the Affirmative's case (ban guns), while the warrant justifies taking that action because banning guns will have beneficial results for the United States. This in-depth analysis is common in both debate rounds and real-world policymaking.

KRITIK ARGUMENTS

Critical arguments, often called "Kritiks," look at the philosophical roots and desirability of policymaking processes and assumptions. These arguments are supported primarily by evidence found in the writings of philosophers dealing with the ethical, moral, and epistemological reasoning and implications behind individual and government actions. For example, the Negative team might present a "Kritik of government coercion" in the ban guns debate. This strategy might include the following argument:

> *Claim:* Government action to ban gun ownership is a violation of human liberty.
>
> *Warrant:* Human liberty is based on the ability to act in accordance with one's wishes and must not be infringed on except in the most egregious circumstances.

The above example uses an analytical warrant to support a Kritik. While this is acceptable, a stronger Kritik would use an evidentiary warrant, citing evidence from a philosopher who has written about the relationship between gun ownership and liberty. An evidentiary warrant is preferable for Kritiks because the philosophers cited have spent considerable time making complex philosophical claims more understandable.

Organizing and Presenting Arguments

Maintaining a logical argument flow is essential to winning a debate round. Before the round begins, teams will determine the order of their arguments. An ideal organization will explain what is happening in the status quo, what will change once the Affirmative plan is enacted, and how those changes will affect society. The early speeches will introduce this narrative; as the round progresses, the team will decide which parts to emphasize and expand in the rebuttals.

Argument Flow

Keeping track of arguments presented in a debate can be difficult, particularly when trying to understand how all of the arguments interact with one another. To reference arguments from previous speeches and different parts of the debate, debaters use "extensions" and "cross-applications." Extending an argument means referencing a previously made argument and explaining how it is still relevant in the debate round. For example, if the 1st Affirmative speaker makes an argument about gun control, the 2nd Affirmative speaker assumes that everyone has heard that argument, and, instead of spending his time restating the argument, he extends his partner's analysis and then presents more warrants to support the claim.

Sometimes extensions increase the intricacy of an already complex argument chain. For example, the 1st Affirmative speaker claimed "guns destroy family life" and supported her argument with evidence from a government report. After hearing the Negative's arguments, the Affirmative team decides that they not only need to provide more evidence about how guns destroy family life, but that they also must prove that family life is worth preserving. Here we have two claims (guns are bad; family life is good) that are integrally related. Both claims build on the original claim, "guns destroy life." The Negative team may respond by answering these new claims independently or by attacking the root claim that guns destroy life. While individual responses will take more of the Negative's speech time, they will also force the Affirmative to spend an equal amount of time responding. In this example, the Negative obtains an advantage because the 2NC/1NR is putting pressure on the 1AR to answer a multitude of varied arguments in a shorter time.

Cross-applications are similar to extensions in that they refer to arguments that have already been explained in the speech or in a previous speech without having to go through a full restatement of the argument. Cross-applying differs from extending because it uses a previously made argument in a different part of the debate than where it was initially made. Sometimes a cross-application can highlight your opponent's logical inconsistencies or provide critical links to powerful advantages or disadvantages. An experienced team will exploit inconsistencies in their opponent's arguments by cross-applying their claims against one another and explaining how an opponent's argument actually supports their side of the debate. For example, the 1AC presented a claim and warrant to prove that "gun control boosts the national economy." The 1NC is planning to make arguments about why improving the national economy will destroy the environment. Rather than spending time proving that the Affirmative improves the economy, the 1NC can cross-apply the 1AC's own argument and then present evidence explaining how economic growth will cause environmental destruction. This method uses the Affirmative's 1AC argument against itself and allows the Negative speaker to spend more time developing his own argument.

How Arguments Are Used in Speeches

To effectively make any arguments, debaters must craft a coherent narrative to tie speeches and arguments together. This process of continually building on an argument encourages argument progression during the round, beginning with claims backed by evidence and ending the round using claims backed by analytical warrants. Even though all speeches must contain arguments made by claims and supported by warrants, each speech in the debate round uses a different balance of analytical and evidentiary warrants. The following outline demonstrates these differences:

The 1st Affirmative Constructive: consists only of warrants from evidence.

The 1st Negative Constructive: primarily uses evidence but can include some analytical warrants.

The 2nd Affirmative Constructive: primarily uses evidence but can include some analytical warrants.

The 2nd Negative Constructive: primarily uses evidence but can include some analytical warrants.

The 1st Negative Rebuttal: can contain evidence that builds on already presented arguments, but cannot contain any new arguments supported by evidence.

The 1st Affirmative Rebuttal: can contain new evidence that responds to arguments made in the 2NC or 1NR but cannot make new arguments with evidence warrants.

The 2nd Negative Rebuttal: should only contain analytical warrants.

The 2nd Affirmative Rebuttal: should only contain analytical warrants.

KEY CONCEPTS

1. All policy debate arguments follow the same structure: a claim and a warrant.
2. Maintaining a common argument structure allows debaters and judges to make comparisons between arguments.

3. Claims are clear, concise statements that summarize the argument. Warrants are reasons why a claim should be accepted.

4. Claims are classified into three types: warrantless, basic, and comparative.

5. Warrantless claims should be avoided because they are statements without any support.

6. Basic claims are statements supported by a warrant that do not attempt to compare an argument to oppositional claims. These are used at the beginning of a debate round.

7. Comparative claims attack an opponent's claim while simultaneously establishing your own argument. They are used at the end of a debate round to draw the judge's attention to specific locations of clash between the Affirmative and Negative arguments.

8. Warrants are the reasons why the claim should be accepted. A warrant may be analytical or from evidence.

9. Analytical warrants support a claim through the debater's own analysis.

10. Evidentiary warrants support a claim by providing a quotation from a published source. This quotation is called "evidence."

11. Policy debate arguments are categorized into three groups:

> *Theory arguments* are used to maintain the rules and norms of the debate. They are intended to maintain an element of fairness and openness in the debate community by ensuring that debaters engage in fair, educational, and respectful practices.

> *Policy arguments* address the pragmatic desirability of the Affirmative plan, most often addressing economic and political considerations.
>
> *Kritik arguments* address the philosophical roots and desirability of policymaking, speaking styles, and debate.[/unl]

12. Debaters organize their arguments to construct a narrative that explains the status quo, the change proposed in the round, and the effects of that change on society.

13. Debaters should build on arguments made in previous speeches by using either extensions or cross-applications.

14. Debate rounds begin with arguments made from evidence and end with arguments supported by analytical warrants.

5

EVIDENCE

"Evidence" is a short quotation used in a debate round as a warrant to support an argument's claim. This chapter introduces the general standards for evidence, the many sources that debaters use to find evidence, and how that evidence is evaluated, organized, and transported to the debate round. A well-prepared set of evidence takes a good deal of time and thinking, making it very valuable. Consequently, this chapter also discusses the norms of sharing evidence within and beyond a squad.

General Standards for Evidence

Policy debate has three standards for evidence.

1. **Evidence must come from a reputable source.** Debate evidence must come from a trustworthy source that is qualified

to speak on the subject. Most evidence will come from peer-reviewed sources such as journals and books. You can also use non-peer-reviewed, publicly available sources, such as government reports, newspaper articles, and online resources. Regardless of the source, you must carefully analyze all evidence for bias, contradiction, clarity, and application to the debate. Wikipedia and other open-source forms of information are not acceptable, nor are items such as the school newspaper, something your mom told you on the phone last night, a Garfield comic, or a blog post. Most important, you should NEVER write your own evidence. Even if you have published an article on the debate resolution, the debate community frowns on using that evidence in a round.

Some teams use evidence from poetry, novels, personal narratives, and music in their rounds. These pieces of evidence may not meet the standards for academic sources; nevertheless, debaters using them must make sure to explain where the text came from, how the text will be used during the debate round, and how using these sources will advance the goals of debate by including new perspectives. These types of evidence are written by people who debaters call "organic intellectuals."

2. **Evidence must be presented in its original form.** NEVER alter the original text of your evidence. Additionally, you cannot paraphrase or use a summary of an article as evidence. Even the smallest change of a word or phrase constitutes academic fraud and is a violation of most university honor codes. Obviously, removing words is also unacceptable.

3. **Evidence must be readily accessible to your opponents.** For evidence to be valid during a debate, you must make a hard copy or digital file available to all participants. Even if you have memorized a particular piece of evidence, you cannot

present it without providing a print or electronic copy. Your opponents and the judge may ask to see your evidence—both to verify that you presented it accurately and to make sure that they understood the argument. Rather than feeling threatened by the request, be happy that your arguments are being carefully considered and reviewed.

Sources of Evidence

Debaters use a wide variety of sources for evidence. While they still use print media, such as books, journals, and newspapers, contemporary debaters also utilize search engines, digital books, electronic archives, and online government sources. Electronic access to resources has improved the quality and specificity of debate evidence while creating a constant race to have the most up-to-date information. Consequently, debaters conduct research before the tournament and then update their arguments between rounds. Debaters most commonly use the following sources:

SEARCH ENGINES

When using sites such as Google or Bing, you should first focus on the terms used in the resolution and then incorporate synonyms into your search. While basic searches are productive, using specialized search engines will greatly improve and hasten your research. For example, Google News is a simple tool for finding only the most recent data. Google Scholar is useful for finding articles from peer-reviewed sources.

JOURNAL DATABASES

Many libraries subscribe to databases that enable patrons to search a wide variety of peer-reviewed publications. When preparing for a tournament, debaters commonly use four databases:

Lexis/Nexis aggregates legal, news, and business publications. Because it contains almost every newspaper in the world, debaters most commonly use Lexis/Nexis to update policy arguments. However, Lexis/Nexis also houses legal journals that are useful for Kritik arguments.

Project Muse is a collection of scholarly journals in the humanities and social sciences. Debaters frequently use this resource to prepare Kritik arguments.

JSTOR is an excellent source for humanities journals, including area studies, political science, and economics. Always use a date limit when researching on JSTOR. The database holds articles from the 1800s that are interesting but will not help your debate argument.

EBSCOhost is subdivided into 31 different databases. For debaters, the most useful subdivision is "Communication and Mass Media Complete," which searches all debate-related articles and is a valuable resource for finding evidence that discusses the values, purpose, and effects of debate. "Academic-Search Premier" is useful for general humanities and science articles, although its holdings overlap JSTOR.

Shrewd debaters do not limit themselves to these databases. Your university may subscribe to hundreds of databases; we encourage you to investigate any that might be tied to your topic.

BOOKS

With increasing access to digital media, debaters less commonly use books to find evidence. This is a mistake! Finding evidence in books may take more time than searching electronically, but books often give a more nuanced understanding of the topic. And, because fewer debaters research from books, evidence from these resources is less common and can provide unique ways of viewing the resolution.

Reading an entire book is not necessary to gather evidence. First look at the table of contents to determine if one or two chapters would be helpful. Then read the opening and closing paragraphs of those chapters. Only if these paragraphs look promising should you read the entire chapter. A different approach is to turn directly to the index and use the terms from your search engine research to find specific references. Finally, look at the footnotes and bibliography, which will point to relevant books, journal articles, and other materials.

THINK TANKS

Think tanks and policy institutes are organizations that conduct research and engage in advocacy on specific issues or policy areas. These organizations, which distribute massive amounts of data, are excellent sources of quality evidence. Because think tanks are supported by organizations with specific political or cultural agendas however, be sure to understand not only the reports that they produce but also the group's motivations for producing them. Realizing in the middle of a debate that your main evidence for an argument is biased by positions that contradict your other arguments can be very embarrassing. You can find think tanks and information about think tank biases by using search engines and examining the article's references. From the references, you will know if the article is based in a particular political point of view, is based only on editorials, or in some other way has only examined one side of the issue.

RSS FEEDS

Really Simple Syndication (RSS) feeds are the easiest way to gather current information because simply by signing up for the service, articles relating to your research topic are automatically delivered to you via email. RSS is exceptionally helpful for long-term research projects. For example, a debater assigned to update evidence on the economy could enter the search terms once and expect an auto-generated flow of information about the economy. Policy debaters use Google Reader and Yahoo! News Alerts to deliver articles to their inboxes daily.

CONFERENCE PROCEEDINGS

Every year, members of policy, research, and academic organizations gather at conferences to speak about their research. Conferences focus on overarching themes, many of which are useful for policy debate. Although some meetings publish their proceedings, many do not. Savvy policy debaters will scan conference programs to find presentations relevant to their arguments and then ask the presenter for a copy of her paper.

GOVERNMENT REPORTS

Government agencies produce an amazing number of reports, some of which are very useful sources of evidence. While the United States does not have a central database for all government documents, a simple Google or Bing search that includes "government publication" will locate these documents.

PROFESSORS

By the middle of the debate season, many debaters have difficulty thinking creatively about an aspect of the topic. Professors can be excellent resources to break through this slump. They are knowledgeable about their subjects, have good research skills, and, since they are not currently involved in competitive debate, they might have a fresh take on the debate topic. Meeting with a professor can produce a better understanding of the topic and win you a few debates. Or, you might have a lesson in how academic professors do not always agree with the arguments debaters make. Either way, professors are usually impressed by the level of research debaters complete and are excited to discuss their own work with interested students.

DEBATE-BASED WEBSITES

A number of websites are dedicated to helping debaters with their research. For example, Cross-X.com and PlanetDebate.com offer free and useful advice on how to conduct meaningful research. If you are starting a new research project, the International Debate Education Association's Debatabase (http://idebate.org/debatabase) has an excellent collection of pro and con arguments that are useful.

DISSERTATIONS, PAST DEBATERS, AND COACHES

After researching a topic for the entire academic year, debaters and their coaches often turn their research into journal articles and dissertations. These publications focus either on debate activities or provide policy analysis of a specific topic from previous resolutions. Although dissertations are not published documents, they often contain the most current scholarship on a topic. At a minimum, scan the footnotes for sources to expand your own research project. Dissertations written by past debaters can be particularly useful because they use the same type of sources that debaters employ to construct their arguments. Dissertations can be searched by using the ProQuest Digital Dissertation Database.

REFERENCE LIBRARIANS

Reference librarians specialize in helping patrons with research. They know where to find the best resources, how to navigate the library's databases, and can offer a variety of suggestions on how to conduct your research. Be sure to consult them.

General Research Strategy

STARTING YOUR RESEARCH

Begin your research by creating a list of key words and terms relating to the topic. Next, use a search engine to find two or three introductory articles that provide an overview of the topic. Use these articles to develop a grasp of the issues surrounding your topic and expand your key word list. As you read, keep a list of issues raised by your introductory articles that would add depth to the body of research. Then, when you have completed your preliminary overview, use this list to collect another, more specific, set of articles.

The ability to think ahead and predict arguments is what transforms an okay debater into a great debater. While researching, attempt to anticipate arguments and find responses. This process begins when you read an article and ask yourself: "How would I refute this argument?" Then, find evidence that supports your refutation.

KEEPING RESEARCH INTERESTING

Debaters do not always love all of their research assignments. However, as they continue to participate in debate, they are able to find creative ways to twist a dull topic into an interesting project. For example, many debaters were disenchanted with the 2008–2009 topic of agricultural subsidies. They made their research interesting, however, by finding ways to tie other topics to the debate. For example, agricultural subsidies determine what foods are cheaply available to U.S. consumers. This, in turn, affects health, habits, and general well-being. Subsidies also determine which foods are grown domestically and which must be imported. This, in turn, directly influences international relations and trade. By investigating the complexity of the topic, most debaters found an area that interested them.

Evaluating Evidence

How does a debater sort through a pile of evidence to find the one piece that will win a debate round? Debaters evaluate evidence based on four criteria: date, source, author's intent, and clarity.

1. **Date.** As a general rule, evidence should be as current as possible. Using evidence from the day of, or sometimes hours before, a debate round is not uncommon. Only Kritik arguments, which address philosophical claims and assumptions, have older evidence. Philosophy classes still talk about Plato, so there's nothing unusual about using philosophical evidence that is decades, centuries, or millennia old.

2. **Source.** Finding an unbiased source is impossible—as is knowing everything about every source presented during a debate. Nevertheless, you should be familiar with the background of the authors who wrote your evidence. When evaluating evidence, ask the following questions:

- Is the author an expert on the topic?
- Is the publication from a NGO, a government document, or a scholarly press?
- What are the publisher's biases?
- Who funded the author's research?
- Does the author have a personal or economic stake in the argument she is making?
- What are the author's philosophical or political leanings?

This information is important because it can help you find contradictions in an opponent's argument and prove the superiority of your own evidence. Each year debaters cite a few authors frequently because of the quality of their evidence. They learn of these authors by examining their opponent's evidence and watching the elimination rounds of major tournaments. The best debaters will then consider how the work of those authors interacts with how their opponents are framing their arguments. Being able to make this type of analysis will quickly win you rounds. For example, the evidence that the Negative team presented might create a logical narrative. But if the Affirmative knows that one of the Negative authors is supported by oil companies and the other works for Greenpeace, they can argue both that the Negative's sources are biased by their funding agencies and that they are inherently opposed to each other's arguments.

The Affirmative can then argue that their evidence, which was written by a more objective scholar, provides the most logical perspective in the round and should be given greater weight when the judge makes his final decision.

3. **Authors' Intent.** A coherent Affirmative case must be constructed from a variety of authors who address the same issue using the same terms. This goal, however, becomes difficult to achieve when authors use the same term in various, sometimes unconventional, ways. For example, the term "weapons of mass destruction" has many different meanings. Some authors may define it narrowly to include only nuclear, biological, or chemical weapons; others may have broader definitions that might include conventional incendiary weapons such as napalm. When conducting research, you must make sure that each of your author's definitions is consistent with your argument.

4. **Clarity.** Clear evidence presents claims and warrants that are easy to understand. This means that the author has used strong wording and been economical with words. Since each debate speech has a time limit, concise evidence that quickly presents an argument is much better than long-winded claims using vague language.

Processing Evidence

The process of turning a quotation into a debate argument is called "cutting evidence." The specific quotation is called a "card" and is extracted from the larger text. A citation, called a "cite," is added. The quotation is then labeled with a one sentence summary called a "tag." The entire product (card, cite, and tag) is then referred to as a "piece of evidence."

Tag →	**New technology is necessary to prevent terrorism**
Cite (Read in-round) →	**Department of Homeland Security, 03**
Cite (not read, but provided for reference) →	(The National Strategy for the Physical Protection of Critical Infrastructures and Key Assets, http://www.dhs.gov/xlibrary/assets/Physical_Strategy.pdf, 2003)
Card (with proper highlighting) →	<u>**We must provide better means of identifying people in order to increase the security of our critical facilities**</u>, systems, and functions. We must create a uniform means of identifying law enforcement and security personnel and individuals with access to critical facilities and systems. <u>**Technologies**</u> to be examined for this authentication scheme <u>**include biometric identifiers**</u>, magnetic strips, microprocessor-enabled "SMART" cards, <u>**and other systems. Such tools would enable quick authentication of identities in the protection and emergency response domains. The enhanced "scene control" entailed would facilitate investigations at the sites of terrorism incidents**</u>, and create an investigative baseline for comparing different analytical data.

TAGS

The tag, which is the first element on a piece of evidence, must be a concise statement that summarizes the thesis of the quotation and states its significance in the debate. Tags should be no longer than a sentence, must be grammatically correct, and should use the active voice. During the debate, you read the tag at a slower pace and with more force than the card. For this reason, tags should be free of abbreviations and should avoid words that are difficult to pronounce.

CITES

The citation includes all of the information your opponent or judge needs to find the evidence and to evaluate the source. You read only a small portion of the citation—usually only the author and year—after the tag and before the card. Citations are created using a standard format that allows debaters to quickly evaluate the information. The following examples indicate all of the information you must include when citing the most commonly used resources. The information read in the round is in italics.

Book
Author's last name, Year
(First name, qualifications, title of book, page number)

Journal
Author's last name, Year
(First name, qualifications, title of article, title of journal, issue number, page number, database used to find article)

Government Report
Government Agency, Year
(Author's name, title of report, page number, web address)

Newspaper
Newspaper Name, Month, Day, Year
(Author's name, title of article, page number, database used to find article)

Government reports and newspapers are cited using the name of the publication rather than the author's name because the authors are often staff or reporters who reflect the perspective of the agency or publication. When making a comparison of report and newspaper cites, knowing that an article was written by Mr. John Smith is less helpful than knowing that it appeared in the *Economist* or was published by the Department of Homeland Security.

CARD

The text of a warrant from evidence is referred to as a "card." The term "card" has carried over from when debaters hand-copied quotes from articles onto note cards. Some debaters now do this by photocopying the necessary page. They then cut out the card, tape it to a piece of paper, and write in tag and cite. Debaters with access to computers scan the original page, cut and paste the card into a Word file, and type in a citation and tag. Some debaters without access to scanners manually type the card into a Word document, but this is the most risky option since it opens up the possibility of leaving out a critical word or phrase.

Highlighting

After cutting the evidence, some debaters underline or highlight key elements of the text to indicate what should be read during the speech. This shortens the amount of text that is presented while preserving the integrity of the original quotation. It is easy to highlight evidence cut electronically by bolding the sections that you will read or shrinking the portions that you will not. These changes are acceptable as long as the font remains legible and the flow of the text is understandable. If you are debating with paper, you may use a highlighter to indicate what portions of the text you will read. Pay attention to the color of your highlighter; yellow and pink are best; purple, blue, or green highlighters will photocopy as thick black lines.

Make sure you are not distorting the meaning of the quote when you highlight. For example, consider the card: *"Dr. Jones reports that more tests are needed because her preliminary results shockingly revealed that no one has ever gotten fat from eating too many candy bars."* Highlighting only *"Dr. Jones revealed that no one has ever gotten fat from eating too many candy bars"* gives a much different impression than reading the entire sentence. Remember that the other team will be able to read the entire card. They will probably catch the distortion, make a fuss about it, and you will lose the round. Furthermore, your judge will witness the event, and soon you'll have a reputation for manipulating evidence.

Experienced debaters will understand arguments well enough to identify the most crucial phrases. These debaters highlight their own evidence and then make copies for members of the squad. Inexperienced debaters often have trouble determining what parts of their evidence they should read. If this is a problem for you, leave the highlighting to a senior squad member or a coach.

Sorting Your Evidence

The best cards in the world will not win you a debate if you cannot find them during the round. Organizing debate cards is a time-consuming process that includes sorting evidence by argument, determining what pieces of evidence are best, throwing away redundant evidence, and creating files that include all of your cards on a specific argument. This is a lot of work but is incredibly valuable because it helps you become familiar with the evidence and know where to find it during the debate round.

The first step in organizing evidence is to determine arguments and subsections. To illustrate the process, let's use the argument topic: Who will win the 2012 presidential election? While conducting research, you will have found a variety of arguments that could be sorted by the candidates, such as Obama, Romney, and third-party candidates. For each of these categories, you will have a pro and a con argument, such as Obama will win and Obama will lose. Within each category, you will have a variety of reasons why Obama might win, which can be sorted into subsections such as "Economy key to Obama victory" and "Economy not key to Obama victory." Make as many argument categories as are necessary to fully understand and debate the topic.

Once you have determined the subsets of the argument, you can begin sorting. If you are working electronically, this process begins by creating new Word documents for each argument subsection and then cutting and pasting the evidence, tag, and cite into the appropriate document. If you are using paper, this process begins by finding a large surface and using Post-it® notes to indicate each argument. You then sort the evidence into the appropriate argument.

Once you have finished sorting, review the evidence in each section and rank it so that the best argument is at the top. Remove all redundant evidence. The best evidence will be from the least-biased source, strongly worded, give reasons why its claims are true, and be based on facts (statistics or empirical studies) rather than analytical arguments.

Frontlines and Extensions

Once you have ranked and organized your evidence, you may begin creating argument frontlines. A frontline is a set of claims supported by analytical and evidentiary warrants used to refute a specific argument. In the past, frontlines were referred to as "briefs" because they are brief collections or presentations of an argument. Good debaters will create frontlines against arguments that they hear frequently so that they can devote in-round preparation time to addressing unexpected arguments. The evidence used in a frontline should be the best from each subsection of the argument.

Extensions are sets of arguments, analytical and evidentiary, that are used to support arguments made in the frontlines. These argument groups consist of the remaining evidence that had been collected for an argument but was not used in the frontline. While the frontline contained a variety of arguments, an extension should address only one of the arguments in the frontline. For example, if your frontline has eight unique arguments, then you should have eight extensions—one for each argument. Extensions are organized with the best evidence first and have few, if any, analytical arguments. Extensions are invaluable during the second constructive speech when your opponent will argue against the quality of your original evidence.

Once the evidence has been sorted into frontlines and extensions, you need to either manually cut and paste the evidence onto a sheet of paper or electronically cut and paste it into a Word document. Each frontline and set of extensions should also be given a title at the top of the page. This title should be a short sentence fragment used to identify the arguments on that page. For example, a title such as "Obama Will Lose—Economy" signifies that the arguments on that page claim that economic issues will cause Obama to lose the election. Extensions to this frontline might be labeled "EXT: Obama Will Lose—Economy." Here "extension" has been abbreviated (EXT) and the title has been shortened to limit the time needed to recognize the subject of the page. The pages in a file should always be numbered to facilitate quick access to the correct argument. This is particularly important for larger arguments, which can have more than 100 pages of evidence.

Creating and Organizing a File

A debate "file" is a collection of frontlines and extensions that support a single side of a single argument. For example, a file titled "U.S.-Russian relations are strong" should contain a frontline of arguments about why the U.S. and Russia are on good terms with one another. If the researcher has had time for extensive research, she might include several frontlines, such as a general frontline titled "Relations strong" or a specific frontline such as "Relations strong now due to technology sharing" and "Relations are resilient." Following each frontline, extensions would be provided for specific arguments from the frontline. If yours is a paper-based team, you would organize files using file folders. In this example, the general frontline of "U.S.-Russian relations are strong" would go in the first folder; "Relations strong now due to technology sharing" would go in the second, and so on. If you debate using a computer, you will create an electronic document for each. Finally, you must put a header on each page that includes the last names of everyone who worked on the file, your university's name, the name of the argument, and a page number.

Files are organized first by the order in which they will be used in the round and second by the type of argument they support. For example, a Negative Politics file would begin with the 1NC argument followed by 2NC frontlines extending specific arguments that were made in the 1NC. Finally, the file would contain extensions to the 2NC frontlines grouped by topic. Similarly, an Affirmative file would first contain the 1AC followed by 2AC extensions and 2AC answers to the most common Negative arguments.

The last step of file organization is creating an index. The index is identical to a table of contents at the beginning of a book; it indicates the title of each frontline or extension and the corresponding page number.

File sizes range from a few pages to an entire ream of paper. For paperless teams, file size doesn't matter; they can be easily searched by a control-F function. However, for paper-based teams, rounds can be won or lost based on the ability to quickly find a single sheet of paper. Small or infrequently used files can be stored in file folders. However, large or frequently used files are commonly organized into Expandos (multiple pocket folders useful for subdividing a file).

Organizing Expandos

Debaters use Expandos to subdivide files such as the Affirmative case and favorite Negative arguments. To be useful, an Expando must contain ONLY one argument or one Affirmative case. Additionally, Expandos must have an index taped to the outside.

Expandos are typically organized first by the order in which evidence will be used in the round and second by topic. For the Affirmative, this means that the 1AC will be placed in the first slot. Then, Affirmative extensions will be organized by advantage areas and use in the round. The back of the Expando will either contain answers to common Negative arguments or will be left empty to allow space for updates to the file. Depending on the size of the Affirmative file, some teams will have two Affirmative Expandos: one for on-case and one for off-case arguments.

For Negative arguments, debaters use one Expando per commonly used off-case argument, such as a disadvantage. The first slot will contain the 1NC frontline. Then, slots will be organized by the frontlines and extensions needed to defend the argument throughout the debate.

Expandos are only successful when they are well-organized and labeled and have a good index. Using shorthand when indexing is helpful for finding information quickly, but everything must be clear and easily decipherable to both you and your partner.

Transporting Evidence

Transporting evidence varies depending on whether you are debating paperless or paper-based. Paperless teams transport their evidence on their computers. They must also bring with them power strips and external hard drives. Paper-based teams carry their files to tournaments in 14-gallon rectangular plastic tubs that hold their file folders and Expandos. Each tub is labeled on the outside, indicating what types of arguments are within. These tubs are sorted first by Affirmative and Negative and then the arguments are identified and organized alphabetically. In addition to indicating the type of argument in each tub, the outsides must be clearly labeled with the team's and squad's name. Tubs are also often decorated with stickers to match the debaters' personalities.

Sharing Arguments and Evidence

Because researching, cutting, and organizing evidence takes a lot of time, debaters are very protective of their files. Consequently, the debate community has developed four standards for using and sharing evidence. Some squads have additional regulations for evidence use; it is your responsibility to understand and adhere to those regulations.

1. **The debater who researched an argument is the first person to present it in a debate round.** No one on the squad can use the argument before the researcher, unless otherwise instructed. This rewards the debater who has completed the research assignment and ensures that the argument will be introduced to the debate community in the most coherent manner possible. This rule applies only to completely new arguments; anyone on the squad may use an updated file.

2. **All team members are responsible for guarding new arguments.** Because new arguments are a strategic way to win rounds, they should NEVER be discussed in public areas at the tournament or the tournament hotel. When discussing new or upcoming strategies at a tournament, coaches typically find an isolated area (a hallway, staircase, or somewhere outside) where they will not be overheard. This secrecy is essential to maintaining a competitive edge. If you have a question or concern about an argument, make sure you are not within hearing distance of a coach or debater from another squad.

3. **Seniority rules.** Usually, arguments researched by coaches are first presented by the most senior debaters. Some squads are obsessive about this and won't even let novices see the argument until the senior team has used it during a debate. Don't get too upset about this restriction. If you haven't seen the argument, you can't be blamed for accidentally sharing it with other squads.

4. **After an argument has been read, you can assume that the entire debate world knows about it and all squad members are free to use it.** Information about arguments travels

quickly because some debaters and judges will carefully record every piece of evidence read during a round and quickly post that information on the Internet. Many of these postings are made on Open Caselist (www.opencaselist.wikispaces.com or www.paperlessdebate.com).

Buying and Selling Evidence

Some debaters are intimidated by other squad members, are overworked, or are just lazy and resort to buying and trading debate files from other squads or private debate research companies. Each squad has its own standards for buying and trading evidence. Consequently, negotiating a sale or trade should be handled by the coach or a senior member of the squad.

Selling another debater's file is unethical. Even selling files that you have researched might violate your squad's policy. Most squads work under the assumption that files created by members are for the benefit of the squad only. To prevent any misunderstandings, always ask a coach before trading or selling anything more than the citation for your evidence.

KEY CONCEPTS

1. Debate evidence is a short quotation used to support arguments. The first four speeches in a policy debate round are primarily used to present evidence supporting a team's position.

2. The three standards for evidence are: it comes from a reputable source, is presented in original form, and is readily accessible to your opponent.

3. Debaters find evidence by using search engines, journal databases, books, RSS feeds, conference proceedings, think tank and government reports, and by speaking with professors, reading dissertations, and consulting librarians.

4. To find evidence, debaters begin with a list of key words, identify the most important arguments to support their position, and then determine which of their opponent's claims require direct refutation.

5. Evidence should be evaluated based on the date, source, author's qualifications, and clarity.

6. All evidence must be clearly labeled with a tag and cite.

7. A tag concisely summarizes the claim and warrants made in the evidence.

8. A cite provides the author, publication name, and date of the evidence so that debaters or judges can find the original source material.

9. Some debaters highlight that part of the text they will read during the debate.

10. Evidence is sorted by the argument that it supports. Then, the best evidence is used for frontlines and supporting evidence is used in extensions.

11. Debate files are created to organize frontlines and extensions for use during the debate round. These may be either paper or electronic files.

12. All members of a debate squad share files. The debaters who prepared the file are the first ones to use it in competition.

13. Although some universities share files and some companies sell debate files to squads, debaters should NEVER buy, sell, or trade evidence without the explicit consent of the head coach.

6

RESPONSIBILITIES OF THE AFFIRMATIVE AND NEGATIVE

The question at the forefront of every debater's mind is, "how do I win?" Policy debate assigns distinct responsibilities and goals to the Affirmative and Negative team to regulate what arguments are presented and how they are analyzed by the judge. Affirmative teams can win the round only by proposing a plan of action that supports the resolution and proves that the advantages of acting outweigh any Negative argument. The Negative team can win only by proving that the Affirmative is flawed. This chapter will address the fundamentals of the Affirmative and Negative. Then, we will turn to the critical question: How does a judge decide which team has won the round?

Being Affirmative

The goal of the Affirmative is straightforward: prove that the Affirmative case and plan are good ideas and better than the status quo. The Affirmative does not have to defend every possible action that the resolution would support; rather, they advocate a specific policy that falls under the realm of the resolution.

HOW DO I WIN ON THE AFFIRMATIVE?

To win, the Affirmative must prove that their case solves specific problems in the status quo without creating any significant adverse effects. The Affirmative proves this position by presenting a series of stock issues, which are parts of the 1AC used to organize and present the desirability of the Affirmative plan. Affirmative teams are required to prove that they meet all five stock issues (inherency, harms, topicality, significance, and solvency) to win the round. For example, when debating the resolution, "Resolved: The United States Federal Government should increase funding to social services," the Affirmative must first prove that problems with social services exist in the status quo. They can do this by presenting evidence that one in six American children are at risk of hunger (harms). Then, the Affirmative must prove inherency: that the current system will not solve the problem. In this case, the Affirmative must prove both that the federal government currently is doing nothing to solve the problem and that it is unlikely to take action in the near future. In this example, if the Affirmative plan calls for giving more children food, the Affirmative must prove that existing programs do not adequately meet the needs of all children. They would support their claim with evidence, for example, statistics showing how many children are at risk of hunger or a statement from the Secretary of Health and Human Services announcing that the federal government will not provide more financial aid for food programs.

After explaining why an action is required, the Affirmative must describe what action they propose. This part of the 1AC is known as the "plan" and is presented as a document that endorses the resolution. Affirmative teams refer to this proposal as the "plan," though it is used to address the stock issue of topicality. For example, consider the resolution "Resolved: The United States Federal Government should increase funding to reduce child hunger in the United States." An Affirmative plan text could be: "The United States Federal Government should increase funding for establishing more food banks serving homeless children."

Once the Affirmative team has presented its plan, they must prove that their action will solve the problem they have identified. These arguments address the stock issue of solvency. In our example, the Affirmative team must explain why and how increasing the number of food banks is the best means for reducing child hunger. While explaining how the plan solves the issues presented in the 1AC, the Affirmative must also explain why their proposal is a large enough change to substantially improve the situation. This explanation involves the stock issue of significance. The Affirmative then backs up their argument with evidence from policy analysts and think tanks. The requirement that a "real-world" analyst has supported the plan ensures that the Affirmative team is proposing a viable and significant idea.

If time remains in the 1AC, the Affirmative team may expand their case by presenting additional arguments, known as "advantages." These set forth the positive side effects of the plan. For example, the Affirmative could argue that, "when children eat better food, they get higher grades in school or are less likely to be ill. Therefore, expanding food programs will improve education and health." Advantages become useful later in the round when the Affirmative needs to compare the effects of the plan with a Negative scenario. While the inherency, harms, plan, and solvency must be presented in the 1AC, advantages can be presented in both the 1AC and 2AC.

Being Negative

The goal of the Negative is to prove that the Affirmative plan does not justify taking action as required by the resolution. The Negative is not responsible for proving that the Affirmative plan is a totally awful idea, merely that it causes more problems than it solves.

HOW DO I WIN ON THE NEGATIVE?

A Negative team has three primary ways to win the round. First, they can prove that the Affirmative is less desirable than the status quo. Second, they can establish that the Affirmative is less desirable than a competing policy. Or, third, the Negative can show that the Affirmative has violated a procedural debate issue. The Negative team can prove their arguments by attacking the Affirmative case, presenting their own alternative plan, arguing against the Affirmative's philosophical approach, or arguing that the Affirmative plan is not topical.

Attacking the case requires the Negative to disprove or at least weaken the claims the Affirmative made in their constructive speeches. If the Affirmative claims to solve child hunger, then the Negative would argue that the Affirmative does not meet one or more of the stock issues. For example, the plan would not meet inherency if child hunger is already being solved, or significance if the plan only feeds a few children, or solvency if the plan will not feed any children. The Negative team can also argue that the Affirmative plan will have negative side effects. These arguments are called "disadvantages" because they present independent reasons why the Affirmative plan is a bad idea. For example, an Affirmative plan that solves child hunger might do so at the expense of increasing the national debt.

Even if the Negative team agrees that the status quo needs changing, they can still successfully argue against the Affirmative by proposing a counterplan—an alternative proposal that solves the Affirmative harms while avoiding the disadvantages of the Affirmative plan. Policy debaters believe that, to be fair, the Negative counterplan must be competitive or propose an alternative way of addressing the same harms or advantages as the Affirmative plan. Additionally, the counterplan and the Affirmative plan must be mutually exclusive, meaning that the counterplan cannot occur simultaneously or as an addition to the Affirmative plan. For example, an Affirmative plan might increase funding to homeless shelters and a Negative counterplan might eliminate homeless shelters. The plan and counterplan are mutually exclusive because the judge cannot simultaneously vote to increase funding for and to close a facility.

Counterplans often work in conjunction with other Negative arguments that seek to attack the pragmatic desirability of the Affirmative plan. In addition to this type of argument, the Negative team can also attack the philosophical construction of the Affirmative plan. Arguments that claim the plan is morally, ethically, and/or philosophically unacceptable are called "Kritiks." This type of argument attacks and questions the ethical, moral, or philosophical merits of the policy issues being discussed and the way in which the debaters have personally conducted themselves while presenting those arguments.

Finally, the Negative team can win the debate by proving that the Affirmative team violated a procedural norm of policy debate. The most common procedural argument is topicality, the argument that the Affirmative proposal does not address the resolution and therefore the Affirmative team should not win the debate, even if their plan seems like a good idea.

Comparing Affirmative and Negative Claims

At the end of a debate round, both teams will have presented a variety of arguments. To clearly explain why their team has won the round and to summarize all of the key issues discussed during the round, debaters use an impact calculus. Provided in the introduction (overview) or conclusion (underview) of rebuttal speeches, an impact calculus proposes and compares standards that debaters want the judge to use in assessing the debate round. The impact calculus has four components: probability, timeframe, magnitude, and impact framework.

PROBABILITY

Probability relates to the likelihood of a scenario. Debaters compare their scenarios by questioning how likely they are to occur. Based on the arguments provided, most judges will say that they find a scenario likely or unlikely to occur. Some judges will even assign probability percentages, saying that a disadvantage might have a 60 percent chance of occurring or, if there's almost no chance, a 1 percent probability. The probability of your argument(s) is determined by clarifying all the different factors that either increase or decrease the chances of an event happening.

TIMEFRAME

Timeframe concerns the amount of time needed for a scenario to occur. For example, the Affirmative claims that passing the Affirmative plan prevents an economic collapse that would otherwise occur within the next month. The Negative claims that passing the Affirmative plan causes a collapse within the next three years. In this case, the judge will vote to pass the plan. A smart Affirmative team will make the judge's decision easier by arguing either that policymakers are sure to figure out a way to prevent economic devastation or that they will have three years to prepare for the collapse.

MAGNITUDE

Analyzing magnitude requires debaters to explain what will happen should the Affirmative plan be adopted and also what will happen if it is not adopted. If the Affirmative proves that passing the plan saves $10 million, but the Negative has proved that the plan will cost $5,000, then passing the plan would have the largest positive magnitude. Magnitude is most often described numerically. This is morbidly known as the "body count" and often results in claims of extinction, nuclear war, or planetary catastrophe. Although gruesome, higher magnitude impacts are typically preferred by debaters because winning a round is easy when their side claims to prevent a nuclear war and the opponent can only claim to save a few lives.

IMPACT FRAMEWORK

How should a judge compare pragmatic, philosophical, and rules-based arguments to determine the winner of a debate? This question has no easy answer; for this reason, debaters will sometimes be required to compare various impact frameworks. Some debaters might argue that saving lives is the most important aspect a judge can vote for. Another team might argue that if the value of life is destroyed, life is not worth living. A good debater will clarify why and how his team's impacts are the most important in the round. Failing to do so means that while your impacts might be larger, more probable, and happen more quickly, you might still lose because the other team has made the case that your framework for the debate is less important.

The best debaters will combine all four types of analysis to persuade the judge. Helping the judge compare your arguments with those of your opponent is exceptionally persuasive. Judges will reward your skill with a team win and high individual speaking points.

KEY CONCEPTS

1. The Affirmative case includes a plan supporting the resolution and reasons why this proposed action is better than the status quo.

2. To win the debate, the Affirmative must prove both that their plan solves a problem and that the advantage(s) of taking action outweigh any problems the Negative identifies.

3. The Negative argues that the Affirmative's plan does not justify taking action as required by the resolution.

4. The Negative may argue their position either by defending the status quo or proposing a counterplan.

5. To win the debate, the Negative must prove one of these four: the status quo is preferable to the Affirmative plan; the counterplan is a better action than the plan; the Affirmative has violated a procedural norm of debate; or the Affirmative has endorsed an unacceptable philosophy.

6. Judges evaluate the round by comparing Affirmative and Negative claims using four criteria: probability, timeframe, magnitude, and impact framework.

7

SPEAKING AND FLOWING

This chapter explains your responsibilities both as a speaker and listener during debate rounds. You might wonder why we haven't titled it "Speaking and Listening." This is because competitive debate requires a unique form of listening and note-taking. Debaters refer to this as "flowing," a skill that allows them to keep track of complex arguments delivered at an incredible rate. Adapting your speech and note-taking patterns to the styles used in policy debate will greatly improve your success as you develop your skills.

Speed and Clarity

Speaking clearly and articulately in the debate round is essential when presenting your arguments to opponents and judges. The best debaters will employ a variety of speaking skills, including pitch, volume, enunciation, and speed. The norms of pitch, volume, and enunciation are similar to any public speaking engagement. However, policy debaters have developed a unique perspective on the speed of a speech. Speed is the most prominent aspect of speech in policy debate.

Many policy debaters speak extremely rapidly. They do this to get as much information into their speeches as possible. While some debaters and coaches frown on speed-reading, the practice is generally accepted and strategically preferred in contemporary policy debate.

Learning to speak at a rate of 400-to-600 words per minute takes time and dedication. Many novices attempt to speed-read at their first tournament, but that's like starting your weight-lifting career by entering the Olympic tryouts. The experience will be uncomfortable and a painful exercise for you and your audience. You need to practice, both at tournaments and in the time between competitions.

Some novice debaters who try to speak faster than they are able end up mumbling. Remember, speaking quickly isn't nearly as important as speaking *clearly*! Some judges will shout at you to be clearer, but don't count on it. When you first start speed-reading, keep an eye on the judge. If she looks confused or annoyed, if she has stopped flowing, or is yelling something that sounds like "CLEAR," then you need to slow down.

If your opponent is mumbling, make sure you get his evidence as he reads it. Also, keep an eye on the judge. If she isn't flowing, she probably can't understand the speaker either. If this is the case, start your next speech by telling the judge to hold your competitors to what the judge could understand. If an argument wasn't delivered clearly, it shouldn't count against you!

You must choose your own ideal speed when speaking; keep in mind that you don't need to speak as quickly as possible to succeed. Although you may have strategic reasons to present more evidence or arguments than your opponents, you must balance speed with quality. Speed demons can be ineffective in their delivery. Use a reasonable rate so that everybody in the round can enjoy and learn. Some debaters speak slowly and carefully construct their (fewer) arguments. Other debaters benefit from lightning-fast delivery because they have trained their minds to keep up with their tongues. As you develop your own style, remember that, regardless of your speed, a speech must always be understandable to the judge and other debaters. Debate is communicative before it is competitive.

Flowing

The rapid speed at which debaters speak has caused competitors to develop an equally rapid means of note-taking. Known as "flowing," this process requires debaters to develop their own shorthand to accurately record and organize the arguments made by both teams. Flowing is an essential aspect of every debate, and each debater must flow all of the speeches that she is not personally giving. Your goal is to record every argument made in every speech. When evidence is provided to support an argument, you will need to record the author and date. Each debater develops a special system of shorthand that enables quick flowing. Regardless of the abbreviations you choose, your flow must allow you to track the progression of arguments, spot holes in your opponent's strategy, and ensure that you can respond to all of the arguments. Every debate team has its own style of flowing, so we cannot help you with the nuances of your partner's style. However, we can offer some useful suggestions to guide you through your first experiences with flow.

Setting Up the Flow

You must use a different piece of paper for every off-case argument and section of the Affirmative case. To set up a flow, use a piece of colored 11x17 paper. Fold the paper vertically into seven columns, labeling each column with the speech name. Column one should be labeled "1AC," column two "1NC," etc. The 2NC and 1NR share a column since they are back-to-back Negative speeches. To help keep the arguments separate, use black ink to record your own arguments and red to record your opponent's. In the upper left-hand corner, label the paper with the argument's title, e.g., "Solvency." Repeat this process for every off-case and on-case argument.

While you do not need to draw rows for your arguments, you should leave approximately one inch of vertical blank space between each argument. This way, if the next speech makes multiple arguments against a single claim from the previous speech, you will be able to record all the arguments without running out of room. You should not run out of space horizontally, but you might run out of space vertically. If so, flip the paper over and keep recording arguments on the back. Some debaters are tempted to use a different piece of paper for extra arguments, but we find that these extra papers get lost or cause unnecessary confusion.

When flowing, record the tag of every argument. Quickly recording tags requires the use of specialized jargon. For example, if the Negative team says, "your plan will lead to a nuclear war, ending all life on earth," you could write "Plan=nuke & extinction." For common parts of arguments, such as a disadvantage, you can use a set of symbols, such as "U" for uniqueness, "L" for link, "!" for impact, and Ø for "does not lead to." You can find a longer list of flow symbols in Appendix C.

Noting when arguments are analytical and carefully and quickly recording the citation for evidence, will allow you to make compelling comparative claims about arguments and evidence presented during the debate. Analytical arguments are only recorded as tags because the debater has created the warrant. However, when the warrant is evidentiary, you also need to record the source of that evidence by indicating the author's last name and year of publication. Here, too, debaters use shorthand. For example, if a piece of evidence was written by Noam Chomsky in 2008, they would write "Chomsky, 2K8." While recording 2K8 is only one character shorter than 2008, it can make a critical difference in a fast round. For cites from the 1990s or 2010s, debaters often use '98 or '11. However, when written quickly '08 looks very close to '98. To prevent confusion, and losing a round because everyone thinks their evidence is a decade older than it actually is, debaters have adapted the 2K_ for the years between 2000 and 2009.

The following illustration demonstrates the design of a paper-based flow for an economics disadvantage. The first 1NC argument was a piece of evidence from CNN. The 2AC responded with a counterclaim from Johnson. Because the Johnson evidence directly responded to the CNN evidence, it was written directly to the right. Because the debater left space between arguments, he was able to record the 2NC/1NR's responses to the Johnson evidence (an analytical extension of the CNN evidence and a Fox News card) directly to the right. This organization has adequately prepared the 1AR to directly answer the previous arguments. When the 1AR begins to prepare her speech, she needs to look at the most recent column (the Negative block). This review reveals several holes. For example, the 2AC impact evidence (from 2006) is much more recent than the Negative's (from 1995 and 2001). To prepare for her speech where she will make comparative claims about this evidence, she needs only to circle the discrepancy.

The Name of the flow goes in the upper left-hand corner.

The 1NC flow is on the far left of the flow.

The 2AC answers to the disad go next to the original 1NC claim.

This is an example of how an individual card or argument appears on the flow. The first component is a short description (tagline) of the argument, in this case "Economic instability leads to global war." Under the tag, we see the citation, in this case, "Mead 95." Many debaters will circle the cite to signify the argument was carded and not analytic. If you don't catch the name or date of the citation, you can put an "X" and fill in later.

ECONOMY DISAD	2AC
Economy stable now (CNN 7/15/12)	1. Non-unique: Economy unstable now (Johnson 7/14/12)
Plan kills auto industry (Hu 2k8)	2. Turn: Plan helps auto industry (Mayer 2K9)
Auto industry key to economic stability (Kim 2k)	
Economic instability leads to global war (Mead 95)	3. No global spillover from domestic economic collapse (Shim 2K7)

2NC/1NR	1AR	2NR	2AR
Extend CNN 7-12—We postdate their evidence More proof—Economy stable (Fox news 7/15/12) Prefer our evidence—plan hurts auto industry Mayer is unqualified (Anderson 2K9) U.S. key to global economy—domestic stability key to world (Mark 2K1)			

Paperless Flowing

Debaters and judges have digitized the art of flowing by using Microsoft Excel to replicate paper-based flowing practices. Many debaters create a template that they can quickly open and use in each round. Like a paper flow, the flow template has seven columns, each labeled with the speech name. All arguments are flowed on separate tabs in the Excel spreadsheet, replicating the one-sheet per argument format of paper-based flow. Although the organizational structure is the same as for a paper-based flow, paperless flows include more full words than abbreviations because many debaters can type quicker than they can legibly write.

Flows After the Round

DO NOT THROW YOUR FLOWS AWAY! Flows are useful records of a round and can be invaluable resources for revising your arguments and improving your debate skills. Immediately after each debate, clearly label your flows with the tournament name, your opponent's names, and the judges' decision. If you flowed on paper, you can fold the papers together and write this information on the top flow. If you flowed electronically, re-title the file to include all this information. For example, if you won a round at Wake Forest University tournament while debating against the University of Pittsburgh team of Smith and Jones in front of judge Mike Mark you could title your file Wake_PittSJ_Mark_win.xls(x).

KEY CONCEPTS

1. Many debaters speak at an accelerated pace. You can acquire this skill through practice or choose to speak at a slower speed and train yourself to address only the most critical arguments.

2. Debate uses a specialized note-taking style called "flowing."

3. All speeches are flowed by all debaters and the judge.

4. Debaters should create a separate flow for each argument in a round.

5. Debate partners should agree on a common set of abbreviations and symbols for flowing.

6. Keep your flows for future preparations, coaching, and argument revisions.

8

SPEECHES

Policy debate's format dictates a strict order and time limit for all speeches, cross-examination, and preparation. This chapter begins by explaining the preparation time each team can use to organize their speeches. Then, it provides an overview of speech order, the types of arguments and their organization during the each speech, and the strategic goals of the debate at each point during the round. Looking deeper into the speeches, we then address the organizational standards of each speech, including the order of arguments, how to transition between arguments, and how arguments are summarized into compelling, round-winning narratives. Finally, we provide a brief overview of cross-examination, the question-and-answer part of each debate.

Preparation Time

In every debate round, both teams have 10 minutes of preparation time ("prep time") to gather their thoughts, organize their speeches, and ask the other team questions that they could not fit into cross-examination. You can use this time before or after any speech or cross-examination period. The team can use it all at once, but most teams take prep time in small increments. In fact, debaters commonly use a little prep time before each speech. You should remember, however, that when one team uses prep time, the other team will be utilizing it as well (although it does not count toward their 10 minutes). Consequently, being quick and efficient with your preparation time is essential.

A preparation period begins when a debater announces to the judge, "we will take some prep time now." The judge keeps track of how much time is used and calculates how much time remains. To ensure accurate recording, debaters must verbally inform the judge *immediately* when they have finished using preparation time.

Because debate partners share preparation time, both partners must agree about when and how to use this period. Begin each preparation session by dividing the tasks that need to be done to prepare for the next speech and determine the order in which you will answer arguments set out in previous speeches. Next, set a time limit for the preparation session and be careful to adhere to it. Many novice teams use the entire 10 minutes to organize constructive speeches, leaving no time for use before the rebuttals. This is a poor strategy because constructive speeches consist primarily of frontlines that are prepared before the debate round. The rebuttal speeches, however, rely on comparing both sides' arguments and require more analysis by the speaker. While constructive speeches do deserve preparation, remember sometimes you may have to begin a speech without having all of the arguments perfectly developed.

Speech Order and Purpose

All Policy debate rounds use the following format:

Speech	Time	Task
1st Affirmative Constructive (1AC)	9 min	Present the Affirmative case, including stock issues, advantages and plan
Cross-examination (CX) of 1AC by 2NC	3 min	Clarify what and how the plan claims to solve; attack 1AC claims
1st Negative Constructive (1NC)	9 min	Present reasons to reject the Affirmative plan
CX of 1NC by 1AC	3 min	Clarify claims from the 1AC and respond to the 1NC claims
2nd Affirmative Constructive (2AC)	9 min	Refute 1NC claims and present additional advantages of the plan
CX of 2AC by 1NC	3 min	Refute and clarify 2AC answers.

2nd Negative Constructive (2NC)	9 min	Present additional reasons to reject the plan, back up previous reasons and refute 2AC claims
CX of 2NC by 2AC	3 min	Refute and clarify 2NC answers
1st Negative Rebuttal (1NR)	6 min	Extend and evaluate previous arguments made in 1NC and 2NC
1st Affirmative Rebuttal (1AR)	6 min	Refute arguments made in 2NC and 1NR and isolate key arguments required to win
2nd Negative Rebuttal (2NR)	6 min	Clarify and present final arguments to reject the plan, compare impacts, and preempt 2AR arguments.
2nd Affirmative Rebuttal (2AR)	6 min	Refute 2NR, compare impacts, and present final arguments in favor of the plan

FIRST AFFIRMATIVE CONSTRUCTIVE—1AC

The 1AC is a pre-scripted speech used to present the Affirmative case. The case presented in this speech forms the basis of the entire round. It identifies a problem in the status quo, suggests a plan of action to solve the problem, and proves why the plan will work. A good 1AC will contain powerful arguments that the Affirmative can extend throughout the debate.

Offense Goals: The 1AC seeks to present reasons for winning the round by offering a number of arguments in support of the plan. While the Affirmative team must be prepared to defend every argument presented in the 1AC, they can narrow the focus as the round continues. Often the debate is won or lost on the basis of just one or two of the many arguments they presented in the case.

Defense Goals: This speech must be strategic and preemptive. It may contain evidence to answer common Negative arguments but should not explicitly predict what those arguments will be. For instance, if the Affirmative case will cost a lot of money, a strong 1AC will include arguments made from evidence that the economic benefits of the case outweigh any initial cost.

Taboo Arguments: Some Affirmative teams think that if they have debated a Negative team at a pervious tournament and already know what arguments the Negative will present, the 1AC speech should be used to answer those arguments before the 1NC even speaks. This strategy is potentially disastrous, however, if the Negative team has adopted a new strategy. *Never* underestimate your opponent—predicting what changes your opponent has made is impossible; thus, the 1AC should only provide minimal preemption for expected arguments. She should go no further than adding one or two new cards to her prepared 1AC speech. This will give the Affirmative a preemptive competitive edge without overfocusing on one possible Negative strategy.

FIRST NEGATIVE CONSTRUCTIVE—1NC

The 1NC attacks the Affirmative plan by presenting a variety of generic and specific arguments. Debaters use generic arguments in almost every round. For example, during election years, they present election disadvantages. These argue that the Affirmative plan will affect who wins the election, thus enabling that candidate to enact bad policies in the future. Generic arguments are usually prepared in the days or weeks before the tournament.

Specific arguments, such as a counterplan or topicality violation, may also be constructed before the tournament but require fine-tuning during the preparation time between the 1AC and 1NC to ensure that they directly apply to the Affirmative case.

Offense Goals: The 1NC has two goals. First, present enough arguments that the 2AC will not have enough time to address them all with in-depth argumentation and analysis. Second, construct several different arguments and impact scenarios that create independent reasons why the judge should vote for the Negative team. Remember the three ways the Negative can win: prove the plan is not better than the status quo, prove the plan is not better than a counterplan, or make theoretical arguments about why the Affirmative should not win. Having several different and independent ways to win allows the Negative team to focus the rebuttals on the strongest argument in the round.

Defense Goals: The 1NC should clearly present several scenarios that support at least one consistent Negative advocacy. A Negative advocacy either argues that the status quo, a counterplan, or a Kritik is a better option than the Affirmative's proposed action. As a novice team, you should commit to one advocacy during the round. This persuades the judge that you have a well-thought-out strategy and that you are not reading all of your arguments in the hope that something applies to the Affirmative. Advancing more than one advocacy complicates later speeches and may cause you to present contradictory arguments or spend much of the rebuttal clarifying your advocacy. For example, a Negative team could present two advocacies: defending the status quo and proposing a counterplan. However, they would then have to devote the bulk of their rebuttal speech to clarifying which they want to advance. Maintaining a clear strategy from the 1NC sets the Negative team up for superior rebuttals that are full of comparisons between the Affirmative and Negative impacts rather than framework explanations.

Taboo Arguments: The 1NC can present almost any argument. However, judges do not respond well to teams that read *every* argument they have in an attempt to overwhelm the 2AC and discourage meaningful debate. Establishing a reasonable number of arguments is a matter of judgment in every round; your decision should be based on the complexity of the 1AC speech and your preparation for specific arguments.

SECOND AFFIRMATIVE CONSTRUCTIVE—2AC

The 2AC must address all of the arguments put forward by the 1NC; any 1NC arguments that she does not answer are considered "dropped" or conceded to the Negative. The 2AC must also maintain the integrity of the arguments deployed in the 1AC and extend important arguments that the 1NC did not refute. Remember, the Negative still has a constructive speech during which they could address any part of the case. By making the extensions of the 1AC and providing additional evidence, the 2AC may preempt these new arguments or at least distract the Negative team from presenting new arguments. If the 2AC has extra time, she can introduce new arguments in support of the plan.

Offense Goals: The 2AC's primary job is to further the Affirmative case. This speech is filled with evidence because it is the Affirmative's last chance to support old arguments and present new ones. The 2AC may also introduce new arguments addressing the specific Negative strategy.

Defense Goals: The 2AC must answer all Negative arguments. If she is running out of time, she may support her claims with analytical warrants rather than evidence. This allows the 1AR or 2AR to expand on those arguments. It is critically important to answer all major arguments in the round. For example, if the 2AC does not address a Negative topicality argument, the

Affirmative will most likely lose the round, even if the team has proved that the case is an overwhelmingly good idea. Most 2ACs minimize the risk of conceding important arguments by answering the most important issues first, then moving on to other Negative arguments. If time remains, the 2AC may attempt to preempt common arguments that the 2NC might introduce in the next speech.

Taboo Arguments: No matter how badly the debate seems to be going, the Affirmative team must not revise the plan or offer a new one.

THE NEGATIVE BLOCK—THE 2NC AND THE 1NR

While the 2NC and the 1NR are independent speeches, the Negative team should fully coordinate both the 2NC and the 1NR before the 2NC speech. This coordination should be the first goal of prep time before the 2NC, following which both debaters will prepare their own speeches. While the 2NC speaker may use a few minutes of prep time before his speech, the 1NR should use very little, if any, time. This division of prep time occurs because the 1NR speaker may use the entire 2NC (9 minutes) followed by the CX (3 minutes) to prepare his speech. These 12 minutes are the longest period of preparation possible in the debate round. This strong coordination enables the Negative to clearly define their strategy and put pressure on the 1AR to answer 15 minutes worth of Negative arguments and 3 minutes of cross-examination in only 6 minutes.

What distinguishes an excellent Negative block from a poor one is how the 2NC and 1NR divide arguments. An experienced team will divide responsibility equally, with the 2NC and 1NR each developing a different argument so well that his speech alone could win the round. This strategy forces the Affirmative to answer both arguments because they are not sure which the 2NR will focus on in her speech.

Poor Negative blocks happen because of two failed strategies. First, the 2NC might take all of the strong arguments. Consequently, the 1AR is able to quickly determine that the 1NR speech has little relevance to the round. Instead of listening closely to that speech, the 1AR will use the time to construct her own speech, tackling only the 2NC's arguments and rendering the 1NR useless. Second, the 1NR might not spend the 2NC speech time crafting his speech. Instead, he will sit quietly during the speech preceding cross-examination and then ask for preparation time to prepare his own speech. This strategy is weak because it shows that the 1NR has no idea how to create his own speech and has to wait for the 2NC's advice. It also allows the Affirmative team additional preparation time to plan answers to the 2NC before hearing the 1NR. The only reason the Negative team should take preparation time between the 2NC and 1NR is if something goes terribly wrong during the 2NC or a problem appears in the cross-examination between the 2AC and 2NC and teammates need to quickly discuss a solution before the 1NR.

SECOND NEGATIVE CONSTRUCTIVE—2NC

The 2NC should defend Negative positions and continue attacking the Affirmative. He can introduce new arguments, especially if the 2AC has just presented something the Negative didn't expect, but often the 2NC simply extends and develops 1NC strategies to reveal their full complexity.

Offense Goals: The 2NC emphasizes the 1NC's stronger arguments while strategically discarding weaker ones. At the speech's finish at least one argument that the Negative can use to win the round should have been firmly established. If possible, the 2NC should present so many good arguments that the 1AR cannot answer them all effectively. Still, the 2NC walks a fine line of providing enough new material to win the round while not providing so many arguments that the explanations are superficial and the educational quality of the debate is diminished.

Defense Goals: The 2NC must answer any 2AC offensive arguments and exploit any weaknesses or contradictions in the Affirmative's arguments.

Taboo Arguments: Reading new arguments is acceptable, but most judges consider reading a completely new strategy abusive because of the time pressure placed on the 1AR. Avoid offering new counterplans, Kritiks, and theory arguments unless absolutely necessary. Judges expect these arguments to have been developed throughout the entire round.

FIRST NEGATIVE REBUTTAL—1NR

The 1NR has two goals. First, fix and explain anything that went wrong in the 2NC. If the Affirmative is going to focus on an argument that was improperly presented during the 2NC, they are likely to hint at their plans during cross-examination. The 1NR should address these issues at the beginning of his speech.

Second, present a detailed, compelling, and eloquent analysis of one or two Negative arguments. This analysis has two goals: 1) make the 2NR's job easier because the judge already has a clear picture of how these arguments function in the round, and 2) put pressure on the 1AR to both answer the Negative's analysis *and* match the rhetorical skill of the Negative speakers.

Remember, the 1NR has both the 2NC speech (9 minutes) and 2NC cross-examination (3 minutes) to prepare his speech. Because the 2NC will be speaking during this period, the 2NC and 1NR must agree on their strategy before the 2NC speech begins. The only reason to take preparation time before the 1NR is if the

2NC did not have time to make a critical argument and needs to explain it to the 1NR so can she can present it in her speech.

Offense Goals: The 1NR's goal is to continue pressuring the 1AR by constructing a complex analysis of how and why the Negative team is winning. Debaters often call this "telling a story" because a good rebuttal will provide a narrative of why the other team is losing and subtly instruct the judge on how to evaluate the round.

Defense Goals: Double-check for any unanswered arguments that the 2NC might have missed. Make sure to thoroughly address any arguments that could lose you the round.

Taboo Arguments: The 1NR MUST NOT present new arguments. This speaker may read a new piece of evidence, but only as an extension to 1NC or 2NC arguments or as an answer to 2AC responses. This speech should focus on making comparative claims with analytical warrants and cross-applied or extended evidence to prove that the Negative's arguments are stronger.

FIRST AFFIRMATIVE REBUTTAL—1AR

The 1AR is like a tourniquet applied on the way to the emergency room. It does not have to hold indefinitely, just long enough to get to the hospital. The 1AR must answer every set of arguments presented during the Negative block and maintain enough of the Affirmative case for the 2AR to prove that the Affirmative has won the round. The 1AR cannot drop arguments, especially if they are (or might become) voting issues. However, the 1AR can save time by using "grouping." For example, if the Negative team presented five arguments about how the Affirmative case will disenfranchise the poor, the 1AR does not need to answer each argument individually. Instead, she can answer the arguments all at the same time. The 1AR can also use grouping to collect useless arguments and quickly explain why they don't matter or were not developed well enough to warrant a response.

The 1AR saves additional time and creates a coherent speech by extending and cross-applying arguments from pervious Affirmative speeches. This strategy of quick cross-application works well when answering disadvantages or a counterplan. Beyond saving time, this strategy creates an appearance of control by allowing the Affirmative team to turn attention back to their arguments rather than seeming to be swamped by the Negative.

Offense Goals: The 1AR must connect Affirmative arguments so that the 2AR can tell a compelling story that supports the plan. She does this by making comparative claims between the Affirmative and Negative scenarios that focus on the probability, magnitude, and timeframe of each team's scenario.

Defense Goals: The 1AR has three defensive goals: 1) extend any theoretical arguments, 2) answer any criticism of the Affirmative's evidence, and 3) introduce more evidence. If the Affirmative has made any theoretical objections to the Negative, they must be restated during this speech. If they are not, they will be considered to have been dropped. Even if the 2AR revives a dropped argument, the judge will not be able to vote on the issue. Similarly, the 1AR must address any Negative challenges to the credibility of the Affirmative's authors. Otherwise, the Negative team can claim that the Affirmative should lose because its evidence is not trustworthy. Debaters might defend authors in other speeches, but they do so most frequently in the 1AR. Why? Because the 1AR, the same person who presented the 1AC, is most familiar with the Affirmative case and can easily refer to that evidence to reference claims and provide argument comparison in the 1AR. Finally, if the 1AR has the time, she should read additional evidence supporting the Affirmative's strongest arguments. This will put exceptional pressure on the 2NR to respond to new evidence as well as create a round-winning narrative.

Taboo Arguments: The 1AR MUST NOT present new offensive arguments. The only exception is when making direct responses to a new argument presented in the Negative block.

SECOND NEGATIVE REBUTTAL—2NR

The 2NR is the last Negative speech. It should evaluate the round and provide the judge with at least one clear reason for voting Negative. Regardless of how many arguments were presented in the round, the 2NR may select only a few winning issues for this speech and clarify why these are more important than those that he anticipates the Affirmative making in the 2AR.

Offense Goals: The 2NR must highlight all of the arguments that the Affirmative has lost and explain why the Negative should win the round. He should then offer what is known as the "even if" scenario. This maneuver explains why the Negative wins the debate even if the Affirmative wins a major argument such as a case solvency argument. For example, a 2NR might use a timeframe analysis to argue, "Even if the Affirmative wins all of their arguments on solvency, we should still win this round because our disadvantage happens quicker."

Defense Goals: The 2NR must preempt the 2AR's narrative. He does this by stressing the superiority of the Negative arguments while making comparative claims against the best Affirmative arguments. The 2NR must make a variety of arguments against all the positions the Affirmative is likely to make in the 2AR.

Taboo Arguments: No new arguments are allowed in this speech. The 2NR may work only with the arguments the Negative has already made in the debate.

SECOND AFFIRMATIVE REBUTTAL—2AR

The 2AR must present at least one reason for the judge to vote for the Affirmative team. A good Affirmative team will have presented several reasons why they might win throughout the round. The 2AR's job is to evaluate all of those arguments, consider the arguments that the 2NR just presented, and select a single winning strategy. This consideration and evaluation should be made using all of the remaining preparation time.

Offense Goals: The 2AR must extend important 1AR arguments that the Negative did not successfully rebut. Then, the 2AR should expand these arguments to present a narrative that explains why the Affirmative team has won the round.

Defense Goals: The 2AR should answer all of the arguments presented in the 2NR. In addition, she needs to resolve any issues that may be confusing to the judge and explain why the Affirmative is superior to the Negative. Because the 2AR is the last speech in the round, it offers the final framing of the debate. This narrative should produce a lasting impression of both the Affirmative's and Negative's arguments.

Taboo Arguments: The 2AR MUST NOT introduce new arguments in this speech. She should work only with the arguments the Affirmative has already made in the debate.

Common Speech Components

While each speech carries specific responsibilities, the policy debate community has three general expectations about how all speeches will be organized and presented. First, each speech after the 1AC will contain a roadmap. Second, all speeches, including the 1AC, will use signposts. Third, rebuttal speeches will include overviews and/or underviews.

THE ROADMAP

The roadmap tells the judge and the other debaters the order in which you will present your major arguments. This very brief introduction occurs before the speech and is not timed by the judge. The roadmap serves only to ensure that everyone's notes are in the same order. Once the judge has organized her notes, she will signal the debater to begin speaking and start a timer to keep track of official speech time. Judges expect debaters to follow that roadmap throughout their speeches.

All roadmaps should indicate exactly how many arguments will be presented in the speech. This allows the judge and debaters to make sure they have enough paper to properly flow the speech. For example, a 1NC who wants to introduce two new arguments on the unforeseen consequences of the Affirmative plan followed by a series of arguments against the 1AC solvency would say: "Two new arguments and then solvency." After presenting this roadmap, the 1NC would wait as the judge organizes her computer files or arranges her paper. At the judge's signal, he will begin his speech.

Policy debate does not have a mandatory order for organizing the arguments in the roadmap; instead, the debaters in each round develop a unique ordering system. Some teams find it easiest to begin by introducing theoretical arguments about the rules and norms of debate. Others put the most important arguments first so they don't have to worry about running out of time. Sometimes a debater has to clarify an argument that was confused during cross-examination, and so that argument is addressed first in the roadmap. Once a team has established an order for arguments, it is best to maintain that order throughout the round. For example, if the 1NC presented topicality first, topicality should continue to be the first argument addressed by the Negative team. The only exception is if an argument must immediately be clarified, for example, if the 1NR needs to clarify a problem from the 2NC. Roadmaps provide a rhythm and expectation for the round. Changing the order of your arguments will send a signal to the judge and your opponents that a problem has occurred in your strategy, so, unless something is wrong, don't change the order.

The first time arguments are presented, debaters will use generic names to indicate the number and type of their arguments. Debaters will indicate an on-case argument for any argument made for or against the Affirmative stock issues. Off-case is used to denote any argument, usually presented by the Negative, that does not directly address a stock issue. For example, the 1NC roadmap might begin with, "I will present two off-case arguments." Using these generic titles allows the judge to follow the speech, but does not reveal specific elements of the argument until later in the speech. Roadmaps that reveal the specific title or argument allow your opponents to begin preparing their answers before you have even started speaking. In our example, your opponents have no idea what off-case arguments you will present—they might be a topicality violation or a disadvantage; they will have to wait until you present each to create a strategy. However, if you presented a roadmap that began, "I will present a topicality violation on the word 'increase' and an economics disadvantage," the Affirmative team can predict what you will say, find their files of answers, and begin to prepare for the 2AC.

The generic name strategy only works before the argument has been presented. In later speeches, these arguments will be specifically named in a roadmap; now the roadmap "I will present a topicality violation on the word 'increase' and an economics disadvantage," is appropriate. This roadmap, which offers greater specificity, allows the judge to differentiate between your arguments.

SIGNPOSTING

Signposting is the continuation of the roadmap that occurs during the speech. It tells the judge that you are leaving one argument and beginning another. Using signposts helps judges and debaters to follow the roadmap. For example, the 1NC might give the roadmap, "Two off-case, the first advantage and solvency." When the 1NC speaker has finished presenting the first off-case argument, he will pause and announce "next off" (which signals that he is going to begin presenting the next off-case argument). The judge then knows to begin a new flow. The 1NC, seeing that the judge has made this transition, will present his next argument. When he has finished, he will again pause and announce a signpost, "on to the first advantage." After the judge signals that her flows are in order, the 1NC will begin presenting his arguments.

OVERVIEWS AND UNDERVIEWS

The primary goal of a rebuttal speech is to create a compelling narrative that explains how the team's arguments work together to win the round. The best way to present this story is by giving an overview and an underview. Overviews are given at the beginning of a speech and underviews at the end. These summaries highlight the most important arguments for the judge and provide a framework for analyzing the arguments made during the speech. This is not a time to make new arguments, but rather highlight a common element in all of your arguments and explain to the judge why those arguments have won the round.

You can use overviews and underviews in any rebuttal speech, but they are most common and most critical in the 2NR and 2AR, when each team must present a compelling narrative about how their side has won the debate. Overviews and underviews are easiest and most compelling when they follow a standard template:

Overview

We, the (Affirmative/Negative) team will win this debate on three key arguments:

1.

2.

3.

Even if you believe our opponents' _____ (insert their best argument here), we will still win the round because _____ (your best argument) beats _____ (their best argument) by _____ (brief explanation of timeframe, probability, magnitude, or framework).

The overview should start the rebuttal speech and will usually take less than 30 seconds. The debater will then use a signpost, such as "now on to the disadvantage," and then follow the roadmap he presented.

Underviews provide a concise reason why you have won the round. Because the judge has been listening to the entire speech, the underview does not need to repeat the overview or a specific argument. Instead, it should quickly remind the judge to vote for your team and highlight the best argument in the round.

Underview

It is clear that we are winning this round on _____ (your best argument).

Even if you believe our opponents' _____ (their best argument)

We have still proven _____ (brief explanation of timeframe, probability, magnitude, or framework of your answer to their argument).

That's it—three sentences. Deliver them clearly and with conviction.

Flowing the Rebuttal Overview and Underview

By the time of the rebuttal speeches, your judge may have run out of paper for the flow. Because you cannot look at the judge's flow during the round but do want to make sure that the overview or underview receives special attention, you may use the roadmap to ask the judge to "take out a new sheet of paper." This request signals to the judge that the overview or underview is valuable enough or long enough to justify a new flow. Even if your judge is flowing on a laptop, you must make this request. For paperless judges, this signals that they must make a new cell at the top of their spreadsheet. Regardless of whether the judge is flowing on paper or a computer, this request ensures that the judge will pay special attention to your analysis and will review that analysis before looking at the line-by-line flow. If you have asked for a new piece of paper for an overview or underview, you must use a signpost during the speech. This signpost might be, "underview, on the new sheet of paper"; it will indicate when the judge should begin to use a new piece of paper.

Conclusion

Knowing how each speech is constructed and contributes to the debate not only helps you prepare your own speeches, it also makes you better prepared for what happens next in the round. Debates don't have free time, and every debater has multiple tasks to accomplish during every moment of competition—even when they have already given all of their speeches. Coordinating with your partner and remembering what comes next will make your debate experience far more fulfilling and successful.

KEY CONCEPTS

1. Preparation time, "prep time," is a 10-minute period allotted to each team for preparing speeches.
2. Debaters must divide their preparation time so that they can prepare for both constructive and rebuttal speeches.
3. Each speech in the debate round has a specific function:

    1AC proposes a plan.

    1NC opposes the 1AC and provides independent reasons to reject the Affirmative.

    2AC defends the plan and answers the Negative's independent arguments.

    The Negative block (2NC and 1NR) splits the Negative's best arguments and explains why those will win the round.

    1AR answers all of the arguments presented in the Negative block and upholds the Affirmative plan.

    2NR extends one or two of the best arguments to win the round.

    2AR proves why the benefits of the plan outweigh the Negative's arguments.

4. All speeches after the 1AC should begin with a roadmap, which informs the judge and opponents of the order of arguments to be presented in the speech.

5. Signposting is used in all speeches to indicate when the speaker is moving from one argument to the next.

6. Overviews and underviews are summaries of arguments used in rebuttals to create a narrative of connections and evaluation between arguments.

9

CROSS-EXAMINATION

In each round, every debater will participate in cross-examination (CX) twice, once as a questioner and once as a responder. This period of questions and answers has two direct effects on the round. First, it contributes to a debater's speaker points, the individual ranking that a judge gives to each debater in the round. CX is a high-pressured and unscripted part of debate and an easy place for the judge to establish rankings among debaters. Second, CX is a strategic part of the debate that clarifies your arguments, breaks down your opponent's arguments, and displays your analytical skills. In this chapter, we will identify the debater's goals as both a questioner and respondent, discuss CX strategies, and summarize what the judge is doing during this part of the round.

Overall Strategy

CX has four benefits: debaters can showcase public speaking and analytical skills, better understand their opponent's arguments, highlight any flaws in their opponent's argument, and indicate specific areas for the judge to evaluate. The judge pays attention to all the speeches, but she cannot ask questions during the round. Thus, debaters try to use CX not only to ask questions that clarify arguments but also to help the judge evaluate the round. If the judge has appeared confused by or disapproving of particular arguments, CX is the time to either provide an alternative explanation for an argument or ask pressing questions that begin to answer your opponent's argument. Don't forget to watch the judge's expressions; often she will signal that a question has been sufficiently answered or that an answer requires elaboration.

Questioner's Goals

When approaching CX, many novices think that they must disprove everything the previous speaker has said. A knee-jerk reaction might be to start yelling questions, not letting the speaker answer or explain his arguments. Don't let him explain, just demand that he say yes or no. Right? Wrong! Please, if you find yourself yelling, stop. CX is not a time for shouting; it is the time for identifying strategic flaws in the previous speech.

Debaters use three types of questions during CX: clarification questions, technical questions, and strategic traps. We have listed these in order of most to least important. If you do not know what just happened in a speech, you will need to spend most of your time clarifying the debate. If you understood all of your opponent's arguments, you have three minutes to find flaws by asking technical questions and setting up strategic traps.

Clarification questions ensure that everything the speaker presented is understood. Don't be embarrassed to ask questions such as, "What was your second argument?" Asking in CX is better than losing on an argument at the end of the round. Beyond clarifying arguments, asking clarification questions can be a strategic way to highlight your opponent's mistakes. For example, if the Affirmative forgot to read a plan text in the 1AC, the 2NC (who is conducting the cross-examination of the 1AC speaker) should ask, "What was your plan text?" Obviously, the 1AC did not present one, but, by asking, the Negative both highlights the error and gets the needed information. The 2NC might worry that she is letting the Affirmative come back from a fatal mistake. However, asking for the plan is better than ignoring the mistake. If the 2NC did not ask for the plan, the 1NC could guess what the Affirmative would have said and answer that imagined argument. This is risky because the Affirmative will most likely present the forgotten plan text in the 2AC, and these Negative arguments might not apply. Asking for the plan allows the Negative to prepare accurate arguments while highlighting the serious error that the Affirmative made in her speech.

Technical questions investigate how a team plans to use their arguments in the round. They should have made this clear during the speech, but if notes are sloppy, the speaker mumbled through his speech, or an argument is confusing, don't be afraid to ask. Technical questions become even more necessary when a speaker has presented several different scenarios. For example, imagine that the Negative team has argued that the Affirmative case will lead to war, environmental pollution, and a plague. Both the Affirmative team and the judge need to know how these scenarios should be analyzed. Is the Negative claiming that war, pollution, and plague will occur at the same time or are they predicting war tomorrow and a plague 20 years from now? The same type of question could be asked of an Affirmative team who presents multiple advantages for their case. Some debaters might not be willing to answer all of your technical questions. That's fine. The judge will notice, and their unwillingness or inability to explain themselves can have a significant effect on who wins the round.

Strategic trap questions are used after all necessary clarification and technical questions have been asked. These questions investigate the speaker's evidence and search for strategic mistakes. Sometimes evidence tags exaggerate the claims of the evidence. Other times, a speaker might make an argument that inadvertently proves the opponent's claim. When this happens, the debater conducting CX can either wait and point out the flaw in the next speech or can ask about it during the CX. If waiting until the next speech, the speaker will have an element of surprise, and the opponent will have to wait to defend her argument. However, if you ask about the contradiction during CX, you can make sure that a flaw does exist in your opponent's argument rather than a simple misunderstanding. If you are sure a contradiction is present, you can use CX to do more harm to your opponent's strategy by framing the question not simply as a "tell me why you read this evidence," but as a string of seemingly harmless questions that eventually lead your opponent into admitting that her evidence does not really support her argument. While these strategic traps can take time and need practice to develop, they are a powerful means of using CX to win a debate round.

Regardless of the questions being asked, all CX sessions should begin by requesting to see all of the evidence read in the last speech. All debaters have a right to review every card that was read during the round. Peruse this evidence carefully and ask questions about specific pieces of evidence. Be careful with this request, however. Teams who are nervous about answering questions will try to spend as much time as possible silently arranging their evidence during cross-examination. Remember, the clock is running and you, as questioner, are in control, so do not allow your opponents to waste time organizing their papers or computer files before answering questions. If you have begun with clarification or technical questions, you can expect your opponents to answer while organizing their materials. When asking strategic trap questions, you need your opponents' complete attention, so make sure that they are not doing anything else like reorganizing their evidence. If they are distracted, they will later claim that they didn't understand your question and retract their answer. This will nullify your trap after it has already been sprung. You can ensure that you have your opponents' attention by simply stating, "This question is very important, could you please stop reorganizing your evidence while you consider your answer."

Respondent Goals

A novice responder might be tempted to make no concessions during CX and tough out the three minutes with "I don't know" and "We'll answer your question in the next speech." This strategy might seem successful because it reveals nothing to the opposing team. However, it annoys most judges. Not answering questions indicates that the debater's arguments are weak or that the debater does not understand his arguments. Rather than stonewall, good debaters view CX as an additional three minutes to expand and clarify their arguments. Additionally, by paying attention to their opponent's questions, observant debaters can determine what arguments the opponent will make in the next speech.

Although you should answer all questions, do not make up an answer and never lie. If you do not know the answer, admit that you are not sure or ask your partner for help. If you are not sure how best to articulate your answer, it is also acceptable to re-read the relevant evidence and take time to consider the text before responding. If the opposing team already has the evidence under discussion, you can ask them to return it to better answer the question.

Finally, never answer a new question while you are still considering the last one. You can only be expected to address one question at a time.

Debaters Not in the CX

All debaters in the round should utilize CX time. If you are not participating in CX, you should first review your flows to ensure that you understand everything your opponent has said. If you find a problem, pass a note to your partner who is participating in CX and have the issue clarified. After all questions have been resolved, prioritize the arguments in the round. Finally, construct answers to your opponent's arguments. When doing so, always begin with the arguments that you are most at risk of losing. This way, if CX ends before you have finished, you will have covered the most important issues your opponent has raised.

CX During the Negative Block

The CX following the 2NC is useful to both the Affirmative and Negative teams. The Affirmative can strategically question the 2NC and the 1NR can prepare his speech. Because this is one of the most competitive moments in the round, some Affirmative teams are tempted to either not ask questions or to ask only a few so that they can end CX early. This strategy is designed to force the Negative team to take preparation time to finish preparing their speech or to give an unpolished speech. Affirmatives who use this strategy are forgetting that while this CX period gives the 1NR three minutes to prepare his speech, it also gives the 1AR three minutes to get ready for hers. Additionally, a good 1NR will have already prepared his speech during the 2NC. Therefore, the Affirmative is not only taking time from their own team but is also losing a valuable opportunity to press the Negative.

Open CX

Any debater can ask the judge to "open CX," which allows all debaters in the round to participate in the same CX session. Some teams prefer to do this before the round starts. Open CX is beneficial when both teams are new to debate and everyone needs to work together to figure out what is going on. However, we recommend that you do not ask for or use open CX unless you need to clarify a critical issue in the round. Open CX can also have downsides: it can distract new debaters from important speech preparation, it can result in haphazard questions, and it can be difficult for the judge to follow.

While having both team members *answering* questions can be advantageous, having both team members *asking* questions is seldom beneficial. Let's use two scenarios to illustrate this point. Let's assume that the First Negative speaker (1N) reads an argument that he does not fully understand but that his partner knows well enough for them to win the round. During CX, the 1A asks questions that the 1N cannot answer. Two things could happen: either the 1N gives a poor response, making the argument look weak, or the 2N asks the judge, "can I use open CX to answer that question?" If the judge agrees, the 2N can answer the question quickly, accurately, and in a way that does not damage the Negative strategy. The 1A might then ask a few more questions, now directed to the 2N, about the same argument. If so, the 2N continues to answer. However, if the 1A starts asking other questions that the 1N can answer, then the 2N can use the remaining time to prepare his speech. In this example, open CX was used quickly and to the team's advantage.

In another scenario, the 2N has a good idea of which arguments he wants to win, but to do so requires a few tricky questions during the CX of the 2A. Traditionally, this is the 1N's CX period and the 2N should be preparing his own speech. However, the 2N is worried that the 1N will not know what questions to ask or will not ask them well. So, the 2N asks the judge if she will allow open CX. The judge agrees and the 2N begins his questions. He should sit down when he has asked his questions and let the 1N take over. However, this 2N continues to ask more questions. His partner, meanwhile, starts a conversation with the 1A. The debaters might be gaining critical information, but they have lost two advantages. First, they are not using the three minutes of CX to prepare the 2NC and so they will have to take prep time after the CX period has ended or give an ill-prepared speech. Second, the judge will have a very hard time following the CX, which will both negatively affect the debaters' speaker points and might also sway the judge's decision. The judge might intervene, asking only the assigned debaters to participate in the CX and the other two to be silent. Or, the judge might stay silent and daydream. If you find yourself in an extended period of open CX, you should immediately stop speaking. Then, apologize to the judge and suggest to your fellow debaters that you return to a standard, two-participant CX format.

Common Problems When Asking CX Questions

The following scenarios address some of the common problems debaters encounter when asking CX questions. These problems can occur on either the Affirmative or Negative side of the debate and deal primarily with CX etiquette, use of time, and how much information to expect from an opponent.

I RAN OUT OF QUESTIONS

As a novice, asking enough questions to fill the entire three-minute CX period can be difficult. Don't panic; you have two good options. First, determine if your partner needs the CX time to prepare her speech. If she does, keep asking intelligent questions, even if they do not set up the arguments she will be making. Ask about the qualifications of your opponent's authors. Take a moment to read a card and ask about those portions not underlined. Fill the time, but do not ask broad questions that allow your opponent to speak at length or make new arguments.

If your partner does not need time to prepare her speech and neither of you has any questions, you can end CX early. But remember, you cannot reopen CX. If you find yourself consistently ending CX early only to think of questions later in the round, take a few seconds of preparation time before the CX for you and your partner to brainstorm a list of questions.

I HAVE ANOTHER, REALLY IMPORTANT, QUESTION

Sometimes, three minutes is not enough time to acquire the information you need for the next speech. If you think you might have too many questions, make sure to begin CX with the most important ones. This way, you will be sure to deal with the most significant issues before time runs out. Additionally, remember that, as the questioner, you should control the CX. If your opponent rambles on, stop him by saying: "Thank you, you've answered my question. I have another question about . . . " Be polite and don't yell at your opponent. The judge will notice if the opponent attempts to circumvent CX and will make deductions from that debater's speaker points.

Even after following this advice, you may have other questions that you don't have time to ask. In this case, use preparation time to ask a question. If you choose this strategy, be sure to consider the following three limitations. First, your opponent does not have to answer any questions asked during preparation time. Second, many judges use preparation time to organize their thoughts, examine arguments, stretch, or visit the water fountain. If the answer to the question is critical, make sure the judge is listening. Third, if you spend a large amount of the preparation time asking questions, you will have no time left to form strategies and organize your thoughts for the next speech.

I HAVE A NEW QUESTION DURING PREP TIME

Occasionally, questions arise during preparation time that could not have been predicted or asked during CX. Usually this occurs after analyzing an opponent's evidence and discovering an organizational issue. For example, two pieces of evidence might be on one page. If the speaker read only one card, you have to ask which card was read. This is as easy as holding up the piece of paper that contains the evidence and asking, "can you mark which card you read?" These types of questions are always permissible and do not require the judge's attention.

Keep in mind that asking questions during preparation time is permissible only during your own preparation time. Asking questions while your opponent is using their preparation time generally is not acceptable. The judge will see this as a deliberate attempt to distract your opponent.

Common Problems When Answering CX Questions

The debater's primary goal when responding to CX is to clarify arguments without admitting to any flaws. If possible, this time should also be used to make an argument stronger. However, occasionally you may not have a strong answer to your opponent's question. This section examines some of these situations and makes suggestions on how even the most confused debater can regain control of the round.

I DON'T KNOW ENOUGH ABOUT THIS SUBJECT TO ANSWER A CLARIFICATION QUESTION

Having a detailed understanding of your evidence before the round is important, but you can't be expected to fully understand all of the elements involved in all of the arguments you will present. For example, a debater claiming, "Egypt will import 10 tanks on Tuesday," can probably answer questions about why Egypt needs the tanks, where the tanks will come from, and who the tanks will be used against. But she might not know certain details, such as why Egypt chose to import 10 rather than 11 tanks. Never guess at an answer; instead, try to take advantage of a clarification or technical question. In this case, rather than saying, "I don't know," point out the weaknesses in your opponent's question. Does it affect the argument if Egypt has 10 or 11 tanks or is the argument based on the fact that Egypt will have more tanks on Tuesday than they do today?

I HAVEN'T REALLY THOUGHT ABOUT IN WHAT ORDER MY ARGUMENTS SHOULD BE JUDGED

Be careful when an opponent asks how various arguments should be evaluated. Your answer will dramatically affect how the judge assesses the round. You should have discussed this issue with your coaches and partner before the round. If you didn't have time to have this discussion, however, don't feel shy about conferring with your partner. This is a very important decision, and, while your opponent might become impatient, your judge will appreciate the thought you are putting into the decision.

SO YOU AGREE THAT X THEORY TRUMPS Y ARGUMENT?

Do not agree to theories that you don't understand! If you don't understand what the question or terms mean, you don't have to agree or disagree. Instead, ask your opponent to define the term or concept before answering the question. Framing your response as "I'll need you to define that term" rather than "I have no idea what you are talking about" makes your opponent explain. This allows you to maintain the upper hand in the discussion and provides information that you can use when answering the argument later in the debate. Most important, this strategy does not reveal your ignorance of the argument. Your opponents will be unsure about the intent of the question—do you genuinely not know what he means or are you just checking to make sure your understanding is the same as theirs.

I WAS STILL ANSWERING THE LAST QUESTION

Sometimes debaters get so excited about asking questions, they don't let you finish your sentences. Analyze these situations before you react. Are you attempting to draw out your answers so that you won't have to face another question? If so, you should expect your opponent to ask you to stop talking. Were you still clarifying a detailed issue when your opponent asked you to stop? If so, you probably need to work on answering more concisely. You also might want to say to the questioner, "this is a complicated issue and I think you might benefit from the entire answer, but if you have a more pressing question, then go ahead." This response signals to the judge that you are trying to explain rather than ramble. Even if your opponent presses on with a new question, you still have resisted the attempt to bully you.

I CAN'T ANSWER THAT WITH A YES OR NO

Some questions, such as, "was your first argument topicality?" only require one-word answers. But others really do need more extensive explanation. If your opponent starts asking questions such as "yes or no, your plan doesn't do anything," find a way to answer that does not begin with a yes or no. For example, you might say, "actually, our plan has five advantages." This is a "no" answer, but signals that you will not be bullied and reminds the judge that you do have five advantages.

CX ENDED EARLY

You are off the hook! Calmly sit down. If your opponent chooses to take preparation time, you and your partner should also take advantage of this time to organize your next speeches. If your opponent is immediately ready to speak, then prepare yourself to flow the speech. Remember that the CX time is controlled by the team who will speak next. If a 2N finishes the CX of the 1A early, the 1A cannot demand that more questions be asked.

Emotions in CX

CX requires debaters to extemporaneously address and analyze issues that are critical to winning the round. When novices are both exhausted and really want to win the round, CX can become over-competitive and stressful. Sometimes this stress results in yelling or crying. If your opponent begins to cry, stop asking questions immediately. You gain nothing by forcing him to continue answering in between sobs. Yes, your opponent might make critical concessions, but the judge is likely to miss these arguments because she is focused on your opponent's emotional distress. Don't press on. Take a moment to acknowledge the tension in the room. Ask an easy question that calms your opponent, even if it doesn't affect the round or your strategy. Then rephrase your important question in a more compassionate way.

If you and your opponent have started yelling at each other, stop talking and catch your breath. Determine why you were yelling and why the issue is so important. Were you just trying to make your voice heard or were you actually upset by your opponent's argument? When the judge evaluates a screaming match, she rewards the debater who stops the yelling. So stop. Rephrase the question or ask your opponent to rephrase his question and start answering again. Sometimes the best way to resolve this kind of escalation is to move on to a different question, revisiting the previous issue later if things have calmed down and time is left in cross-examination. Finding a way to deescalate the situation will help you make your argument clearly, make it easier to interact with your opponents, and also be well-received by the judge.

KEY CONCEPTS

1. Cross-examination (CX) is the only period of direct question and answer between debaters during the policy debate round. CX has strict time allocations (3 minutes) and occurs after each constructive speech.

2. Cross-examination provides an opportunity to showcase analytical and speaking skills and has a direct impact on individual speaking points.

3. Answers to CX questions are binding; teams frequently reference information garnered from questions and answers in debate speeches.

4. Debaters must answer questions during CX but do not have to do so during prep time.

5. Use all of the CX time. This gives your partner three minutes of preparation time for her next speech and gives you more practice asking questions.

6. CX questioners should begin with clarification questions, followed by technical questions, and then strategic traps.

7. CX responders should try to avoid strategic traps while attempting to use as much time as possible to further develop their arguments.

8. Debaters not in the CX session should use the time to prepare their speeches.

9. Use open CX, with the judge's consent, for short periods of the CX session and only to clarify specific arguments.

10. Like all parts of the debate round, CX should be engaging and non-abusive. Under no circumstances should debaters force their opponents into an overemotional state.

10

THE 1AC

The First Affirmative Constructive (the 1AC) is the first speech of the debate. In this speech, the Affirmative presents their case for defending a specific plan of action, supported by evidence, that falls within the year's resolution. Policy debate uses four types of 1ACs: policy, Kritik, hybrid, and performance. Your squad might have specific regulations about what type of 1AC you will present, or you might be free to select an option for yourself. Either way, you will eventually have to debate against each type of 1AC when you are Negative, and those debates will be easier if you understand each type of Affirmative case. This chapter discusses the goals of the 1AC as a speech and the distinction between each type of 1AC. It then offers examples and outlines of each 1AC type to illustrate their differences and use in the round.

Goals of the 1AC

The 1AC is a pre-scripted nine-minute speech that sets the stage for the round. During this speech, the Affirmative lays out a series of justifications for a specific plan. These justifications are known as the Affirmative case and are used to illustrate how the Affirmative will be defending their plan. Because of the time required to prepare the speech, teams usually present the same 1AC all year, making small changes to ensure that their arguments are up-to-date.

The 1AC has four goals:

1. **Explain how the Affirmative will defend the resolution by offering a plan that advocates a specific action to address the problem highlighted in the resolution.** The plan is a short declaratory statement, typically no more than a few sentences, that will be the focus of the debate. The rest of the 1AC will provide a series of justifications for the actions proposed in the plan.

2. **Identify how the plan solves the problems relating to the resolution.** This requires finding evidence from qualified sources that explains why acting in accordance with the plan would resolve issues pertaining to the resolution.

3. **Offer multiple advantages to adopting the plan.** These advantages should provide a variety of reasons for adopting the plan and give the Affirmative a set of impact scenarios to use against upcoming Negative arguments.

4. **Preempt Negative arguments against the plan's ability to solve the problems.** This goal is optional. Preemptive arguments safeguard the Affirmative case against the arguments that the Negative will present. You should attempt preemption

only if time allows and if you have a reasonable understanding of what the Negative will present in their 1NC.

The 1AC is *not* responsible for proving that the plan would have enough support to be passed by Congress. Policy debate utilizes the term "fiat," to explain that the Affirmative and Negative teams and judge will assume that the plan will be passed by Congress (or adopted by another government agency if specified by the resolution). This allows debaters to debate if the plan *should* be passed instead of if it *will* be passed.

Choosing Your 1AC

Plans can be incredibly different despite each one relating to the resolution. Consider the following four plans, all prepared by the same squad for the 2007–2008 resolution:

> Resolved: That the United States Federal Government should increase its constructive engagement with the government of one or more of the following countries: Afghanistan, Iran, Lebanon, the Palestinian Authority, and Syria, and it should include offering them a security guarantee(s) and/or a substantial increase in foreign assistance.

Based on this resolution, the squad prepared the following plans.

> *Plan 1:*
> The United States Federal Government should increase its constructive engagement with the government of Afghanistan by providing foreign assistance for judicial reform to the Ministry

of Rural Development and Health of the Afghan government.

This plan proposes a very specific form of constructive engagement with only one of the nations listed in the resolution. A team using this type of plan does not try to solve all of the problems set forth in the resolution and prefers to have a narrowly focused debate about a specific Afghan agency.

> *Plan 2:*
> The United States Federal Government should promise not to attack or to overthrow the Iranian regime on the condition that Iran agrees to restore diplomatic relations, including allowing the United States to open an embassy in Tehran.

Plan 2 is much less specific than Plan 1. Plan 2 is phrased as an offer and an exchange between the United States and Iran. While it sets a condition for this offer (an embassy in Tehran), it does not include the specifics of how that embassy would be built or how the United States would ensure its promise to not attack Iran. By proposing this plan, the Affirmative signals that they would like to debate the broader implications of the resolution, not the specific details of the plan.

> *Plan 3:*
> The United States Federal Government should increase its constructive engagement with the Islamic Republic of Iran by offering a security guarantee in the form of a treaty pledging that the United States will halt all efforts to impede Iran's development of nuclear technology.

Plan 3 differs from Plans 1 and 2 because it is one-sided. The United States will offer a treaty that only governs the behavior of the United States. The Iranian government is the passive party to this treaty. This type of unilateral United States action is easier to debate because the Affirmative has to prove only that the United States will uphold its offer, they do not have to prove that Iran will accept the offer or participate in any way.

> *Plan 4:*
> We affirm the resolution as a metaphor for the need to acknowledge the people of Palestine through compassionate dialogue and to abandon the notion of Otherness.

Plan 4 is very different from the previous plans. Plan 4 is a critical or Kritik plan that takes a philosophical approach to the resolution. This plan signals that the Affirmative would like to debate the philosophical presumptions and assumptions made by policymakers and the effects of those presumptions and assumptions on the people of Palestine. Instead of simply saying that we need to look at the philosophical reasons behind our actions, Plan 4 outlines a specific method of philosophical investigation, compassionate dialogue, and the reason for that action—to abandon the notion of Otherness.

Each Affirmative plan presents a different policy, but they all uphold the resolution by calling for constructive engagement with one of the countries listed. These examples illustrate the different levels of specificity and creativity a plan may have as well as the differences between two general types of plans: policymaking and philosophical.

How Do Debaters Choose a Plan?

Most teams begin developing their plans by reading about the topic and finding policy proposals currently being discussed by experts in the field. They then brainstorm possible plans to produce a list of options that they can research to determine the most feasible. They might also find a few new ideas while conducting their research. They can either choose one of those new options or make a note of them and return to those ideas later in the debate season when they want to try something new.

While conducting your research, look for the answers to the following questions:

1. Has your idea been tested in another country, debated in Congress, or tried by a court? If so, what was the result?
2. Do any existing laws or regulations prevent your plan from being executed?
3. Who would the plan help? Who would it hurt?
4. Who are the major academic, government, and philosophical supporters of the plan?

The answers to these questions will give you a good idea of the strength of your potential Affirmative case. Choosing which plan and case are right for you can be difficult, but remember that you can always change or improve your case as the year progresses.

Novice debaters are rarely asked to create a plan by themselves; instead, novices are expected to become familiar with the strategies provided by the coaching staff and senior team members. Then, when they ready, novices can begin offering their own suggestions.

Components of the Affirmative Case

To create an Affirmative case, debaters begin by determining what evidence they will need to support their plan. As they conduct research, they create two piles of Affirmative evidence: evidence that might work well in the 1AC and evidence that will be used for 2AC extensions. Potential 1AC evidence is further organized into the general areas of a 1AC: inherency, harms, significance, plan, and solvency. To see how these sections come together, let's look at how a 1AC might be constructed to support the resolution, "Resolved: The United States Federal Government should provide humanitarian assistance to North Korea."

Inherency explains that the present system is not solving the problem. For example: the United States has cut all ties with North Korea.

Harms explain the implications of not taking action. For example: cutting ties with North Korea prevents food aid from reaching the country, resulting in millions suffering from malnutrition and starvation.

Significance quantifies the harms and justifies focusing on a particular problem in the round. In our example, the significance is "millions suffering" as opposed to one or two individuals. The 1AC rarely mentions significance explicitly; it is usually implicitly incorporated into solvency.

The plan text is a short statement of the proposed policy. For example: The United States Federal Government should provide food aid to North Korea.

Solvency explains how and why the plan will be successful. For example: By providing food aid to North Korea, we solve one of the key causes of aggression.

This example 1AC outline demonstrates the difference between the Affirmative's requirement to address each of the stock issues and the way an Affirmative case is presented in the 1AC. The stock issue of topicality is replaced by the plan and only discussed if the Negative team presents a topicality violation that argues that the Affirmative does not relate to the year's resolution. Additionally, while this example clearly separates each of the five components, many teams choose to organize the Affirmative case by grouping together two or more of the stock issues. This organization produces a logical flow to the 1AC and allows the Affirmative to use evidence that addresses multiple stock issues at the same time.

Organizing the Affirmative Case

Affirmative teams can organize the components of the 1AC speech in any way they prefer. However, we recommend that new debaters select one of the two classical formats outlined below. The first style organizes the speech by each of the five stock issues. During the debate, each component, except for the plan, is labeled an "observation." These components are integral, individually labeled, and individually argued parts of the Affirmative case.

Style 1:

Observation 1: Inherency

Observation 2: Harms (includes significance)

Plan

Observation 3: Solvency

The second style utilizes an "advantage." The advantage combines harms, significance, and solvency into a scenario that the Affirmative case will solve. In the second style, only inherency is referred to as an observation; advantage(s) are referred to by advantage and a number.

Style 2:

Observation 1: Inherency

Plan

Advantage 1: (includes harms, significance and solvency)

Types of 1ACs

Policy debaters use four types of 1ACs: policy, Kritik, hybrid, and performance. Some debaters choose a style at the beginning of their debate career and never change. Others experiment with all of the styles. Even if you have already determined which style you like best, you need to understand each style to adequately prepare for Negative rounds.

Let's examine each of the four types of 1AC as they could be debated. For the first three examples, the plans will focus on the resolution:

> Resolved: The United States Federal Government should substantially reduce the size of its nuclear weapons arsenal and/or substantially reduce and restrict the role and/or missions of its nuclear weapons arsenal.

Please remember that a real 1AC is a 10-to-30 page document, full of long quotations (evidence) and arguments. We have only included the tags of the evidence and a brief description of the evidence that would be used during the debate round so that you can see the general organization of each 1AC type and not get bogged down in the individual arguments. Since the tag provides the thesis of the evidence, the argument should be clear. The tag lines might seem awkwardly worded or appear to be missing critical information, but they are written to maximize the presentation of information quickly and efficiently. For full text examples of 1ACs used in debate rounds, consult opencaselist.paperlessdebate.com.

Policy

Policy 1ACs present a plan that proposes a single policy option that meets the resolution. These policies are those that could be adopted by a government agency, debated in Congress, or ruled on by a court. A policy 1AC focuses on the political implications of the plan. It usually contains contemporary evidence and claims to solve for harms such as genocide, nuclear war, or extinction. These impacts are often quantified to estimate how many people the plan will affect. The following is an example of a policy 1AC that reduces the size of the U.S. nuclear weapons arsenal by phasing out all Trident missiles (nuclear missiles launched from submarines).

This 1AC uses Style 1 outlined above. It has an inherency observation followed by three harms observations, the plan text, and then a solvency observation.

Observation 1—Inherency

1. The U.S. currently deploys 260 submarine-based nuclear warheads in its fleet.
2. These weapons, known as Trident warheads, are incredibly unstable.

Observation 2—Harms: Accidental Detonation

1. Trident warheads are accident-prone—even small shocks could cause detonation.
2. Accidental detonation causes nuclear war and extinction.

Observation 3—Harms: The Food Chain

1. Inferior casing design makes Trident warheads prone to leakage, risking irradiation of the ocean.
2. Ocean radiation contaminates the food chain.
3. Food chain contamination will cause extinction.

Observation 4—Harms: Russia

1. Russia maintains a high-alert status in response to the threat of the U.S. Trident system. High-alert status risks accidental launch from radar glitches and human error.
2. Accidental launch would spur all-out conflict and nuclear war.

Thus the plan: The United States Federal Government should dismantle its nuclear Trident warhead arsenal.

Observation 5—Solvency

1. Eliminating the Trident warheads is critical to preventing accidental detonation—no other action can solve the case harms.
2. Dismantling the Trident warheads solves the risk of ecological disaster.
3. Russia will lower its alert status only if the United States eliminates its Trident warheads.
4. Acting now is critical to solving for these Trident missile scenarios.

Dividing the harms into three observations is a smart Affirmative strategy. This organization allows the Affirmative team to argue that their plan prevents three separate scenarios: accidental detonation, nuclear contamination of the ocean, and accidental conflict escalation resulting in the launching of nuclear weapons. Later in the round, the Affirmative can choose to continue with all of these scenarios or they can focus on only one or two. By separating the harms into different observations, this policy 1AC also forces the Negative to debate three different scenarios. This organization is particularly useful if the Negative focuses on the political, pragmatic ramifications of the case rather than focusing on a Kritik. You can typically determine the types of arguments a Negative team is likely to present by using opencaselist.paperlessdebate.com to find out what they have done in previous rounds.

Kritik

Kritik 1ACs present a philosophical criticism of policymaking. They might propose a specific action that the government could take, but rather than expect that the policy would hypothetically be implemented, they use the plan text to criticize the status quo. While Kritik 1ACs use the same components and organization as a policy 1AC, the evidence, the evidence tags, and the plan text are radically different. Kritik 1ACs are less concerned than policy 1ACs with estimating the number of people who will be directly affected by the plan. Instead, Kritik Affirmatives seek to identify the root cause of the problems identified by the resolution and offer a philosophical analysis of how to address these harms. For example, while the policy 1AC identified the risk of accidental Trident missile launch as a harm, a Kritik 1AC might instead seek to change the mentality that created the need for building

Trident missiles. Because Kritik 1ACs deal with philosophical harms, they often offer philosophical solutions, such as calling on debaters and judges to change the way that they think about the resolution. Given the complexity of these arguments, tags for Kritik evidence tend to be longer and more complex. While policy 1ACs tag their evidence with short declarative sentences, Kritik tags can be as long as a paragraph and contain both narrative and explanation.

The following Kritik 1AC, based on the nuclear weapons resolution, argues that the United States has become obsessed with nuclear weapons, viewing them as a god rather than instruments built by humankind. The structure of a Kritik 1AC is usually far less rigid than that of policy 1AC. As with the following example, most Kritik 1ACs provide a narrative structure divided into "contentions" or subheadings. The speech begins with contentions that include multiple stock issues to support a similar argument. Then the plan text is presented, labeled only as "Plan Text." Finally, solvency is often presented as an individual contention.

Contention 1: God Mode

- The United States has come to see its nuclear arsenal as a new god, able to protect us as long as we believe in it. This belief has produced a dichotomy that posits the United States as absolute good and our enemies as absolute evil. This perspective encourages us to strive for supremacy at any cost, which necessarily dehumanizes our enemies and allows us to use any means necessary to destroy them.

- Our attempt to maintain nuclear superiority leads to increased militarization, which makes nuclear proliferation and war inevitable.

- The terminal impact is extinction—the militarization of society destroys all life on Earth.

Contention 2: Disposable Populations

- The deification of nuclear weapons has turned humans into disposable commodities; we are mere cogs in the capitalist machine of militarism. The way in which we conceptualize nuclear weapons influences how we treat others. So long as we aim nuclear weapons at other populations, we signal that it is acceptable to sacrifice lives for our economy and security.

- Furthermore, this machine mentality is the bedrock of the capitalist value system.

- This perspective leads to extinction—the logic that allows us to sacrifice certain parts of the population justifies the destruction of an entire population.

Thus the plan: The United States Federal Government should eliminate its nuclear weapons arsenal and ban the use of nuclear weapons.

Contention 3: A Way Out

- The plan is key to ending the chilling effects of nuclear weapons on the world's population.

- Taking small steps toward eliminating nuclear weapons is not an option—Cold War activism proved that piecemeal reduction and reform are not enough.

- Only the plan solves—the mere existence of nuclear weapons sustains the mentality that justifies genocide and makes extinction inevitable.

This Kritik 1AC prepares the Affirmative team to defend only one position during the round: the total elimination of nuclear weapons. While this limits the Affirmative's options, it also gives the Affirmative team a major advantage over Negative strategies such as disadvantages that argue that the plan hurts the economy or prevents a politician from winning an upcoming election. Kritik Affirmatives spend time constructing an in-depth explanation of the philosophy they intend to debate. This preparation allows the 2AC to respond to almost any policy-based argument that the Negative team makes by attacking the Negative's philosophical assumptions about the resolution.

Hybrid

Hybrid 1ACs use a policy proposal to evaluate ethical observations about systemic problems (those that affect the entire world) such as human rights violations or environmental sustainability. Hybrid Affirmatives use an organization and plan text similar to those used by policy and Kritik 1ACs. However, the evidence used to support these arguments is a blend of policy and Kritik sources. Many hybrid 1ACs separate the policy and Kritik evidence into different advantages.

The following hybrid 1AC is a strategic option for a team that wants to present a predominantly policy scenario but also wants to leave open the possibility of crafting a critical strategy based on ethical issues. In this example, the first observation, "Nuclear War Termination," contains inherency, harms, and significance to support a policy argument. Observation Two, "City Busting" (a term used by those who study nuclear weapons policy to signify the use of nuclear weapons on civilian city centers) includes inherency, harms, significance, and solvency to support a Kritik argument.

Observation 1: Nuclear War Termination

1. Conventional wars are inevitable. However, as long as nuclear weapons are on alert, the United States risks being pushed to the brink of using nuclear weapons. (inherency, harms)

2. The United States is likely to use nuclear weapons to end present conflicts. (inherency, harms)

3. Limited nuclear use destroys U.S. deterrence—this ensures extinction. (harms, significance)

4. Even the threat of war increases the likelihood of nuclear miscalculation and encourages other states to use nuclear weapons in conventional conflicts. (harms, significance)

5. Use of even a single nuclear bomb on a heavily populated area will spark massive retaliation because countries become convinced they will be exterminated. (significance)

Thus the plan: The United States Federal Government should prohibit the use of nuclear weapons on cities.

Observation 2: City Busting

1. The atomic bombings of Hiroshima and Nagasaki epitomize human violence and immorality—hundreds of thousands of innocent people were killed even though less destructive strategies to end the war existed. (inherency, harms)

2. City-busting destroys entire population centers indiscriminately—it reduces civilian causalities to mere numbers and justifies the worst atrocities imaginable. (harms, significance)

3. Failure to oppose this kind of violence ensures human extinction—we have a moral obligation to resist using nuclear weapons to slaughter civilians. (harms, significance)

4. Justifying the loss of lives through calculative logic makes war more probable in the future. (significance)

5. Keeping the option of city-busting on the table is the moral equivalent of dropping the bomb. (significance, solvency)

This hybrid 1AC is well-positioned to answer both policy and critical arguments. Depending on the Negative's strategy, the 2AC may choose to maintain the variety of arguments or he may use only the critical or policy elements. Although many hybrid teams will collapse their strategy to only policy or only Kritik, some prefer to keep both options open through the 2AR. This strategy forces the Negative team to strike at two different targets. Additionally, keeping both options open can be useful when debating before a panel of judges. Some judges prefer critical arguments, while others prefer the policy option. Providing a variety of ways to vote for the Affirmative will make it easier to win more judges' ballots.

Performance

Performance Affirmatives combine policymaking with the rhetorical skills of public speaking in an attempt to engage the audience. Performance and Kritik Affirmatives are not always easily distinguishable, but the performance 1AC will generally devise a more performance-based presentation such as dancing, singing, or speaking in multiple languages. While performance teams may offer a plan, they may also critique the debate community or the political process for using rhetorical standards, jargon, and expectations for evidence to specifically exclude underrepresented and oppressed populations. Performance 1ACs are innovative and still considered a new approach to policy debate.

They highlight that the rules and norms of the debate community are constantly changing in an effort to expand the means of communicating.

For the inexperienced debater, these 1ACs can be difficult to understand because they do not draw on evidence from traditional sources. Performance 1ACs can be exciting, however, because they put special emphasis on drawing the audience into the debate.

To explain performance 1ACs, let's examine the 2010–2011 resolution:

> Resolved: The United States Federal Government should substantially increase the number of and/or substantially expand beneficiary eligibility for its visas for one or more of the following: employment-based immigrant visas, nonimmigrant temporary worker visas, family-based visas, human trafficking–based visas.

In 2010–2011, performance Affirmatives were popular because debaters wanted to focus on the cultural norms that are used when determining who is awarded a U.S. visa. Of particular concern to these debaters is the common practice of denying visas to gay individuals; accordingly, they often assume a different identity (that of a straight individual) or forgo immigration to the United States. In the example below, the Affirmative team has taken issue with this process and its philosophical basis (heteronormativity) and carefully chosen their terms. They have opted to use the word "queer" instead of other terms such as "gay." This decision was made based on the academic literature known as "Queer Theory," a branch of critical theory that examines the intersections of sexual orientation, gender identity, and culture. Additionally, they have chosen to say "perform a different identity" rather than "adopt a new identity" since most

Queer Theory literature argues that all forms of identity are merely performances, not true representations of the self. From this perspective, the 1AC argues that true equality and freedom, qualities that the United States aspires to, are impossible as long as visa regulations are based on heteronormativity.

Drawing on the rules and norms of the debate community, the following example also identifies collegiate policy debate as a place where heternormativity discourages queer individuals from participating. The 1AC strategically argues that rules such as topicality stem from the same preconceptions used to discriminate against queer persons in the visa process. Performance Affirmatives typically employ this strategy in an attempt to draw individual debaters and their actions into a larger discussion of how the year's resolution applies to our collective daily lives.

Beneath these arguments, the performance 1AC uses the same organization as a policy or Kritik 1AC. The speech begins with an introduction (covering inherency, harms, and significance) followed by an advocacy statement (plan text), and conclusion (containing solvency). However, in an effort to streamline the presentation, performance 1ACs do not usually label the observations (such as inherency and solvency). The performance 1AC evaluates impacts in the same way as a Kritik 1AC—by addressing the root of the harms.

PERFORMANCE 1AC

1. Frances Wright, a 19th-century reformer and immigrant to the United States who worked for the emancipation of slaves, once said that without equality there can be no liberty. Unfortunately, U.S. immigration policy isn't equal. We, as intellectuals, as debaters, and as human beings, can no longer be ignorant of the oppressive practices of U.S. immigration policy.

2. The United States, claiming to be an "equal nation," has entrenched itself as the sole regulator of immigration and social norms, thus giving the government ultimate control over the public at large.

   Our opponent will most likely stand up and respond to our case by: a) presenting a contrived hypothetical situation that claims treating all migrants as equal will lead to nuclear war or b) complaining about some dubious postmodern concern. We will argue, however, that our thoughts and scholarship should be evaluated first in this round. We believe that treating some migrants as more equal than others is a clear act of dehumanization.

3. For individuals seeking a U.S. visa, the only option is to adopt the normative American lifestyle. Immigrants are forced to become part of an oppressive society that rejects anything that does not conform to its social structure. This is heteronormativity—a social structure that calls for the normalizing of all individuals into predetermined gender and social roles.

4. This process of forced assimilation feeds upon itself, making the system of immigration increasingly normative. We are terrified by the similarities between this process and the heteronormative demands of history's most repressive regimes. We will argue that continual forced assimilation makes violence, hatred, and war inevitable.

5. Policy debate constructs narratives of immigration and visa politics within normalizing standards of theory, predictability, switch-side debate, and state focus. All of these standards determine acceptable traits in our community. Debaters pretend to rule over the immigration system, applying normative structures that influence each of us as we play the game of academic deliberation. We, as individuals, must come to terms

with the debate ballot serving as our own form of visa protocol. What fits the norm is voted for and thus accepted.

6. We advocate the rejection of these heteronormative standards within the immigration system and the debate community. The judge should view the round as a means of rejecting the current standards used to determine the winner of the round and should, instead, determine a winner based on personal acceptance of the gay migrant. (This is the plan text.)

7. Today, in this round, we are the queer migrant. Only by dropping all limits that bar the Other from existence in the debate round, only by becoming the queer migrant can we truly accept the immigrant as a legitimate person and reclaim humanity.

8. Our advocacy has two parts. First, we believe that sexuality scholarship must rethink the process of migration and how that process changes our personal roles. Second, we believe that queer immigration scholarship must challenge the normative presumptions of sexuality that are produced within systems of power and immigration.

This performance 1AC prepares the Affirmative to argue against both Kritik and policy arguments. If the Negative team decides to present only policy arguments, the Affirmative team will be able to focus on the evidence presented in the second argument and offer extensions to prove that heteronoramtive visa regulations make way for other encroachments of state power. If the Negative team chooses to focus on Kritik arguments, the Affirmative can rely on the sixth, seventh, and eighth arguments—that until we change our philosophical framework, none of the U.S. policies can be considered free or equal.

While the 1AC is presented as a performance, the 2AC and later speeches do not also have to be performances. Each performance team develops their own style after the 1AC. Some will continue with narrative speeches. Others will begin to argue in a style similar to a policy team (reading large amounts of evidence and engaging policy topics) and only reference their previous performance. Teams determine which strategy they will use after evaluating the Negative's arguments.

Affirmative Disclosure

The variety of 1AC styles and plan texts can make preparing for the Negative side of the debate difficult. Clear debates occur when both teams understand what is going on, and so the policy debate community has developed the norm of Affirmative disclosure.

On request, the Affirmative team will provide the Negative with their plan text and the generic details of their advantages or observations. The Affirmative is not expected to give the Negative team a complete copy of the 1AC, though they may choose to answer questions about the evidence they will present. Whatever information the Affirmative elects to share is exchanged as soon as the teams know that they will be debating against each other in the next round. Sometimes disclosure occurs five minutes before the round begins, sometimes it occurs an hour before the round. After receiving this information, the Negative team will meet with their coach and develop a general strategy for the upcoming round. Any printed materials that the Negative borrows during disclosure (such as a copy of the plan text) must be returned before the round begins.

The community has two exceptions to the disclosure norm. First, if the Affirmative is presenting a completely new Affirmative (both the plan text and advantages are new), they do not have to disclose it so that they can maintain the element of surprise. In this case, when the Negative team asks for disclosure, the Affirmative simply says, "it's a new Aff." This strategy works only once. After a team has read the 1AC, they must disclose it to all future Negative teams. Second, the Affirmative can withhold new advantages. If the Affirmative team is presenting an old plan text but a new advantage, they must disclose the plan text and old advantages but may say they have "one new advantage." Affirmative teams are not required to say anything else about the new advantages.

Why do Affirmative teams disclose their 1AC? First, there is no point in trying to hide a 1AC. Internet case listings, such as those offered on Paperless Debate (http://opencaselist.paperlessdebate.com/xwiki/wiki/opencaselist/), make 1ACs readily available. In contemporary debate, disclosure simply ensures that everyone will start the round with an accurate understanding of the 1AC. Second, Affirmative teams are usually prepared to debate very specific elements of their plan. Well-focused debate cannot occur if the Negative team spends the entire round making generic arguments. Disclosure enables the Negative to develop a strategy for debating specific issues in depth. Third, all Affirmative teams must also debate the Negative side of the resolution, so Affirmative disclosure eventually helps all teams since debaters tend to share information. The debate community has collectively decided that Affirmative disclosure is a good idea. While teams will not be directly penalized for refusing to disclose, judges may perceive those teams as unfriendly or their arguments as weak and unable to stand up to a tougher Negative strategy.

KEY CONCEPTS

1. The Affirmative's goal is to present a viable plan that affirms the resolution.

2. The goal of the 1AC is to frame the plan by providing proof that it will both solve the immediate harms of the resolution and will have a number of positive side effects (advantages).

3. 1ACs are selected based on research and debater interest. The 1AC is a pre-scripted speech that is written and practiced before the tournament.

4. The 1AC includes five fundamental sections: inherency, harms or advantages, significance, plan, and solvency.

5. Affirmative cases must meet the stock issues of inherency, harms, topicality, significance, and solvency. However, they do not have to explain how these burdens are met unless asked by the Negative team.

6. The four kinds of 1ACs are: policy, Kritik, hybrid, and performance.
   a. Policy 1ACs focus on the policy-based solutions enacted by the U.S. federal government.
   b. Kritik 1ACs focus on philosophical questions relating to the resolution.
   c. Hybrid 1ACs include both policy and Kritik attributes, allowing debaters to focus on either option in the rebuttal speeches.
   d. Performance 1ACs engage the resolution by offering a plan but might also focus on critiquing the debate community or the political process in general.

7. The debate community presumes that the Affirmative teams will disclose their plan text and advantage areas before the round (unless the Affirmative is reading a completely new 1AC or advantages for the first time).

11

THE NEGATIVE STRATEGY

The goal of the Negative team is simple: successfully challenge the desirability of the Affirmative plan. Negative teams may achieve this goal by using three strategies (status quo, alternative policy, and rejection of the resolution) and four types of arguments (topicality, disadvantage, counterplan, and Kritik). This chapter explains how Negative teams select and utilize frameworks and arguments and offers an overview of each type of Negative argument.

Three Negative Strategies

By choosing a strategy before the round begins, the Negative team can make sure that their arguments do not contradict one another and that they will be able to clearly explain to the judge why the Negative has won the debate round. The Negative has three strategy options: support the status quo, argue that an alternative policy is better than the Affirmative plan, or contend that the resolution is flawed. In this chapter, we will study each strategy by using the resolution:

> Resolved: The United States Federal Government should substantially increase its development assistance, including government-to-government assistance, within the Greater Horn of Africa.

DEFENDER OF THE STATUS QUO

Traditionally, the Affirmative defends the resolution and the Negative defends the status quo. Using this strategy, the Negative has to prove either that the Affirmative plan causes more harm than good or that the Affirmative has not proved that their plan solves their harms.

Assume an Affirmative team presented the following plan: "The United States Federal Government should increase the amount of development assistance to Tanzania." The Negative team might argue that the United States already gives aid to Tanzania and increasing the amount of aid will have no effect on the harms or will cause significant, deleterious side effects.

PROPOSER OF ALTERNATIVE POLICIES

Negative teams who agree that the status quo needs to change can propose an alternative policy. Debaters call these proposals "counterplans." The goal of a counterplan is to prove that the Negative has a better policy option than the Affirmative's plan to solve the harms.

For example, if the Affirmative plan is "the United States Federal Government should increase the amount of development assistance to Tanzania," the Negative could present a counterplan: "the United States Federal Government should increase the amount of development assistance to Kenya." This debate would then focus on why the Affirmative chose to devote resources to Tanzania rather than Kenya and why giving aid to Kenya is preferable.

REJECTER OF THE RESOLUTION

Negative teams opposed to the entire annual resolution (including the Affirmative case) are called "rejecters of the resolution." These Negative teams justify rejecting the resolution by criticizing a specific word in or the entire philosophical foundation of the resolution. For example, the Negative team might deem development aid "colonialist" and take issue with the aid the resolution requires.

Selecting Arguments

After selecting a strategy, the Negative team develops a variety of arguments. Most Negative teams begin the round by presenting multiple arguments in the constructive speeches and then narrow the number down to one or two of the best arguments in rebuttal speeches. In the constructive speeches, this procedure enables the Negative to find weaknesses in the Affirmative's case and ensure that the Affirmative is so busy answering arguments that they have little time to present additional arguments of their own. In the rebuttal speeches, the Negative limits their own arguments so that they make a detailed and comparative analysis of both why they have won the arguments and how their arguments have mitigated the Affirmative's case.

Regardless of the strategy, Negative teams use two classes of arguments, specific and generic.

Specific arguments focus on the Affirmative plan. If the plan calls for the United States to increase its technology imports from Japan, the Negative team offers specific arguments against those technologies or against increased Japanese imports. These arguments are hard-hitting and designed to test how well the Affirmative understands specific elements of the plan. The more specific these arguments are, the stronger they will be. To be competitive through an entire year, specific arguments must be varied and constantly updated with new research.

Generic arguments apply to any Affirmative that meets the resolution, but they do not address the specific Affirmative plan. If the plan calls for the United States to increase its technology imports from Japan, the Negative might offer arguments against increased imports to the United States (but not specific to Japan or technology). Generic arguments are very strategic when the Negative is not sure what the Affirmative is planning to say before the round begins, for example, if the 1AC is new and your squad did not have time to research a strategy against this specific team.

Some teams prefer to use generic arguments in all rounds because they don't have the resources to prepare specific arguments against every team. Or, they might want to take advantage of the in-depth knowledge they have gained from focusing on a specific argument. For example, a Negative team that argues that any action in the resolution would destroy the global economy would be extremely well-versed in the subtleties of the financial system. Yes, the Affirmative might be able to predict that Negative teams will argue about the global economy, but it is unlikely that the Affirmative will be as prepared for economic arguments as the Negative, who dedicate nearly all their time to that type of argument.

Try to use both argument classes to ensure that you have a wide variety of arguments that can keep the Affirmative on their toes.

Types of Arguments

The most common Negative arguments are: topicality, specification, disadvantages, counterplans, and Kritiks. Each type is used both offensively and defensively against the Affirmative case. Arguments are referred to as "offensive" when they both put pressure on the opponent and provide a specific reason that the opponent has lost the round. Arguments are defensive when they maintain the team's position and prevent the team from losing the round.

TOPICALITY

Topicality arguments, referred to as "violations," accuse the Affirmative of violating the wording of the year's resolution. The Negative argues that the Affirmative plan is outside of any reasonable interpretation of the resolution. The Negative can only be expected to debate about the resolution.

Offensive: Topicality violations argue that the Affirmative has been unfair and that a judge cannot vote for an unfair team.

Defensive: The Negative team uses the Affirmative's violation of topicality to explain why the Negative team could not predict that they should research the case and has, therefore, been unfairly disadvantaged by only being able to present generic arguments.

SPECIFICATION

Specification violations force Affirmative teams to clarify how their plan will be enacted. The Negative team uses specification arguments to claim that the Affirmative has failed to specify the nuances of their plan, making the debate vague and unfair. This argument is presented in one of three ways:

1. Agent specification (A-spec) argues that the Affirmative has failed to specify *who* will execute the plan.

2. Implementation specification (I-spec) argues that the plan text has failed to specify *how* the plan is to be implemented and/or enforced.

3. Over specification (O-spec) argues that the Affirmative plan has provided excess detail, making it too technical to understand or debate.

Just as with topicality, specification arguments are prima facie (Latin for "first view" or "first in order") reasons for the judge to reject the Affirmative. Offensively, specification violations argue that the Affirmative should lose for failing to provide necessary information about their case to the Negative team at the beginning of the round. Defensively, these arguments prevent the Affirmative from later clarifying the case in a way that undermines the relevance of the Negative strategy.

DISADVANTAGES

Disadvantages outline specific adverse effects of passing the Affirmative plan. These scenarios could be political, economic, or social. A Negative team can present a variety of disadvantages in the same round as long as they don't contradict one another.

Offensive: Disadvantages argue that the 1AC will have serious negative side effects.

Defensive: Disadvantages claim that the status quo is superior to the 1AC plan because it prevents the scenarios the plan will cause.

COUNTERPLANS

Counterplans are alternative policy proposals that either change the way the 1AC is enacted or propose a different policy that solves for the Affirmative harms without causing Negative side effects.

Offensive: Counterplans compete with the Affirmative plan by proving that there are other, superior ways to solve the harms.

Defensive: Counterplans allow the Negative to argue that they have a better policy than the Affirmative.

KRITIKS

Kritiks are philosophically based criticisms of the resolution, the Affirmative's policy proposal, or the Affirmative's behavior during the round. Kritiks frame the debate round in one of three ways:

1. As a debate about the philosophical ramifications of a specific policy action.

2. As a debate about the ideological assumptions underlying policymaking decisions.

3. As debate about the how debaters should interact during the round and then use their skills to affect the world of policymaking.

Offensive: Kritik arguments attack the Affirmative's theoretical ground.

Defensive: Kritiks argue that the judge should vote Negative in support of a superior theoretical framework.

The best Negative teams understand the fundamentals of each Negative argument. They will be prepared to use every type of argument during the round, but will have come to a consensus between partners about which arguments they like best. Affirmative teams should keep notes about which arguments Negative teams most often present and which ones they tend to focus on at the end of the debate so they know how to debate the Negative team if they face them again. Consequently, Negative teams either need to be exceptionally good at one specific argument (so even though Affirmative teams know that will be the round-deciding argument, the Negative will still win) or the Negative team needs to create a unique mixture of arguments for each round and be willing to go for whatever argument best rebuts the Affirmative plan and best suits the judge's preferences.

KEY CONCEPTS

1. The Negative must determine its strategy: status quo, alternative policy, or criticism before the round.

2. The most common Negative arguments are topicality, specification, disadvantages, counterplans, and Kritiks, all of which can be used offensively and defensively.

3. The Negative should combine a variety of arguments in its constructive speeches and then focus on the best in the Negative rebuttals.

12

STOCK ISSUES

"Stock issues" refer to the parts of the 1AC used to organize and present the desirability of the Affirmative plan. Affirmative teams are required to prove that they meet all five stock issues (inherency, harms, topicality, significance, and solvency) to win the round. In this chapter, we will define each of the stock issues, explain how they 1AC presents them, and how the Negative team argues against them.

The Five Stock Issues

Policy debate has five stock issues:

> **Inherency** explains the current conditions that have led to and perpetuated the problems that the plan will attempt to solve.

Harms identify problems that justify the plan.

Topicality requires that the plan address the resolution.

Significance requires that the plan be important enough to have caught the attention of government analysts or academic researchers.

Solvency proves how the plan will cure the harms.

While Affirmative teams must win each of these stock issues, they do not always have to debate each issue. If the Negative does not address a stock issue, the judge will assume that the Affirmative has met the requirements of that issue.

The Negative has an easier job; they need only prove that the Affirmative has failed to satisfactorily address one of the stock issues. This unbalanced requirement is called the "Affirmative burden." Any potential unfairness of the Affirmative burden is resolved by the speech order because the Affirmative speaks both first and last in the round.

Let's look at each stock issue to understand how the Affirmative proves and the Negative disproves it.

INHERENCY

Inherency proves that there is a reason why the Affirmative plan has not yet been adopted and is not likely to be implemented in the future. This stock issue ensures fair division of ground and prevents Affirmatives from proposing plans that the federal government has already adopted or is about to implement.

Debate separates inherency into two types: structural or attitudinal. To explore the difference between types, let's use the resolution:

> Resolved: The United States Federal Government should substantially reduce the size of its nuclear weapons arsenal and/or substantially reduce and restrict the role and/or missions of its nuclear weapons arsenal.

Structural inherency proves that a law, court decision, treaty, regulation, or some other legal barrier prevents policymakers from addressing the harms. When debating our example resolution, the Affirmative team can prove that they are inherent by presenting evidence that the START I treaty, which limits strategic weapons including nuclear weapons, expired on December 5, 2009.

Attitudinal inherency indicates that the Affirmative plan has not yet been enacted because policymakers or interest groups are opposed either to solving the problem or taking the action the Affirmative proposes. When debating the nuclear weapons resolution, the Affirmative could prove attitudinal inherency by presenting evidence that the general public does not want a new START treaty and that congressional approval of new treaty limiting nuclear weapons is impossible without public backing. Attitudinal inherency does not require the Affirmative to claim that their plan is unpopular—they merely have to show that no one is interested in resolving their harms.

When evidence exists to prove both structural and attitudinal inherency, Affirmative teams usually present structural evidence. They do so because structural inherency proves that a legal barrier prevents their plan from being implemented, but does not suggest that anyone actually opposes it. In contrast, attitudinal evidence proves that a group is specifically opposed to change. While this meets the requirement of inherency, it puts the Affirmative in a difficult position because they have admitted that a group would oppose their plan.

Negative teams can argue that the Affirmative violates inherency in two ways. First, they can attack the Affirmative's structural inherency by presenting evidence that the plan has already been enacted. This strategy has become increasingly rare because the Internet provides ready access to the most current information on specific legislation or court rulings, but when it is employed it is damaging. More commonly, Negative teams attack the Affirmative's attitudinal inherency as part of a detailed strategy that requires the Affirmative to prove that their plan is unpopular. This Affirmative concession will support the Negative's disadvantages that argue the plan's unpopularity will cause adverse effects. This strategy takes advantage of the Affirmative's attitudinal inherency that claims that the plan is unlikely to be implemented because it is unpopular. The Negative then concedes that the Affirmative is inherent and uses the Affirmative's own responses to prove that the disadvantage is true.

The Affirmative team replies to the Negative's argument by conceding that their plan is unpopular. This does not necessarily mean an immediate loss for the Affirmative. The Affirmative can still win the round if they prove that their plan's advantages outweigh the Negative's disadvantage.

HARMS

Harms are events that have or will have adverse affects on society, domestic politics, and sometimes the entire world if the plan is not enacted. Harms can be predicted (a problem is developing) or contemporary (the problem already exists). For example, in March 2010, teams were reading harms evidence about the potential for oil spills in the Gulf of Mexico and claiming that their plans would prevent an oil spill. On April 20, 2010, the Deep Water Horizon drilling rig exploded, resulting in an enormous oil spill. As a result, debaters changed their arguments. The harm was now contemporary, and teams had to change their plans from preventing to controlling an oil spill.

The Affirmative team must present plausible and specific harm scenarios. For example, a harms scenario predicting that England will attack the United States is extremely unlikely and would not make a good argument. A better scenario could predict that al-Qaeda is seeking to attack the United States in the near future. Harms scenarios that predict terrorism will happen in an unspecified country in the next 10 years are not specific enough to encourage good debate.

The Negative team can argue against the Affirmative harms in two ways. They can make analytical and evidence-supported claims that the harms have been exaggerated or will be solved by another means. Or, they can use the harms to justify a Counterplan. The Counterplan accepts the Affirmative harms but argues that policies other than the Affirmative plan could better solve the problem.

TOPICALITY

All Affirmatives must be "topical," meaning that they address the year's resolution. The Affirmative proves topicality through the plan text. If the proposed plan addresses all elements of the resolution, it is topical. For example, responding to the resolution "The United States Federal Government should substantially reduce the size of its nuclear weapons arsenal, and/or substantially reduce and restrict the role and/or missions of its nuclear weapons arsenal," the Affirmative might offer the following plan: "The United States Federal Government should substantially reduce the size of its nuclear weapons arsenal by dismantling all warheads on B-2 bombers." At first glance, this plan might seem topical because it calls for a number of weapons to be dismantled. However, a bit of research will show that even though the United States has equipped a number of B-2 bombers to launch a nuclear weapon, no actual warheads are on the bombers. Therefore, this plan is untopical because it does not decrease the actual number of weapons.

The more vague the resolution, the easier it is to be topical. For example, the 1980–1981 resolution, "Resolved: That the United States should significantly increase its foreign military commitments," made determining topicality easy: does or does not the plan increase foreign military commitments? However, resolutions have become increasingly complex, often including a list of treaties or specific portions of policy to be addressed. These resolutions require the Affirmative plan to endorse a very limited number of policy options.

Negative teams argue that Affirmative cases are not topical by presenting "topicality violations." These are pre-structured arguments consisting of analytical arguments and one definition which claims that the Affirmative has violated the resolution and as such created an unfair debate. For example, consider the plan text that calls for the dismantlement of all nuclear weapons equipped on B-2 bombers. A Negative topicality violation against this plan would start by providing a definition that to reduce the arsenal is to remove existing weapons from service. Next, the Negative would argue that the Affirmative violates topicality by proposing a plan that results in no actual action. The rest of the violation would clarify why this is unfair to the Negative and justifies the judge voting Negative without considering the pragmatic implications of the plan.

SIGNIFICANCE

Significance addresses the size and scope of the Affirmative plan. This stock issue ensures that the Affirmative is proposing an action large and meaningful enough that it is debatable, i.e.

arguments can be made both in support of and against the plan's proposed action(s). For instance, a plan that decreased defense spending by $20 is not significant, but one that decreased defense spending by $20 billion is.

Determining what is and is not significant depends on how the debate resolution is worded, how the words in the resolution are defined, and if an authoritative body of literature exists on the topic to ensure a fair debate for both sides. Determining significance can be a difficult. For example, considering body counts could be a measure of significance since every human life is inherently important. Yet a small number of deaths might not qualify as significant because they may not have gained enough attention from mainstream media, government officials, and academics to generate a balanced amount of literature for both sides. Making the argument that saving a few lives is insignificant does not imply that these lives don't matter, it does contend that not enough literature exists to have a fair discussion.

The plan is assumed to be significant unless the Negative team argues otherwise. Negatives challenge significance by providing a definition of significance within the context of the resolution and then explaining why the plan does not meet that definition. They might also support their definitions with analytical and evidence-based arguments that compare the significance of the Affirmative plan with other policy options.

The Affirmative would respond to this challenge by offering a competing definition of what qualifies as significant and then offering evidence that reliable sources have discussed the Affirmative plan. This evidence could come from a government document or a national newspaper but not from obscure Internet blogs or tabloid newspapers.

SOLVENCY

Solvency ties the Affirmative case together by explaining what will happen after the plan is passed and what advantages will come from that action. Solvency arguments begin with evidence proving that the plan will remedy specific harms. Next, the Affirmative presents evidence indicating that this specific type of action has significant advantages over both the status quo and any arguments the Negative is likely to make. Solvency evidence is usually derived from policy analysts or government officials who have suggested the plan. Typically, solvency is the most important part of an Affirmative case since it proves that the Affirmative plan can effect long-term change.

The stock issues—inherency, harms, topicality, significance, and solvency—are the basic components of any Affirmative case. Although Negative teams cannot predict every argument that the Affirmative will present, they can expect that the Affirmative will attempt to meet the demands of each stock issue. By crafting generic arguments for each, and specific arguments when possible, the Negative team will be prepared for any round. Because Affirmative teams must meet each stock issue to win the round, the Negative team can concentrate on the Affirmative's weakest argument and make a strong argument for their side.

KEY CONCEPTS

1. The five stock issues are: inherency, harms, topicality, significance, and solvency.

2. The Affirmative must win each stock issue to win the round. The Negative only need disprove one stock issue.

3. Inherency explains the current conditions that have led to and perpetuate the problems that the plan will attempt to solve.

4. Harms identify the problems in the status quo that justify the plan.

5. Topicality requires that the plan meet the resolution.

6. Significance requires that the plan be cogent enough to have caught the attention of government analysts or academic researchers.

7. Solvency answers how the plan will alleviate the harms.

13

TOPICALITY

As we have learned, topicality is the stock issue that debaters use to determine if an Affirmative plan is within the scope of the year's resolution. Limiting the scope of what the Affirmative plan can propose is important to maintaining competitive fairness and educational value during a debate round. While these are subjective values, debaters have created a detailed set of standards to evaluate what the Affirmative can and cannot propose during the round, and what the Negative should and should not expect from the Affirmative's case. Any Affirmative who violates these standards will lose the round—a harsh but necessary penalty. Debaters value the preparation that occurs before a debate round, and that preparation can only occur if a team can predict their opponent's arguments.

This chapter introduces the basics of topicality, discussing how Affirmative teams interpret the resolution when constructing a plan and how Negative teams predict what the Affirmative will advocate. It also discusses specification theory, a set of arguments that focus on the level of information the Affirmative team must provide about how their plan will be enacted. Topicality and specification theory are separate arguments, but both use the same standards of evaluation and address the same concepts of fairness and education in the round.

Topicality Basics

Topicality is the most important stock issue because it limits what the Affirmative can propose and ensures that the Negative has a reasonable chance of arguing against them. Negative teams claim that topicality is a prima facie voting issue. The judge must address topicality first because it dictates whether the Affirmative is relevant to the resolution and, by extension, if the round has been fair to both the Affirmative and Negative teams.

Before the debate season begins, squads create a list of possible Affirmative cases. This list is referred to as "predictable cases," those that a well-informed researcher could derive from the resolution. This list might not include all possible Affirmatives, but it does provide the Negative with a general idea of what is probably topical so they can prepare arguments against these cases. When a Negative team encounters an Affirmative case that is not on this list, they will likely present a topicality argument.

Topicality from the Affirmative Perspective

A topical Affirmative case includes a plan that falls within the resolution's limits. The Affirmative creates this plan by researching the definition of each word in the resolution. These definitions may be taken from a standard dictionary, but debaters prefer definitions provided by policy experts or government documents because they explain how real-world policymakers would discuss the resolution. From these definitions, the Affirmative team and their coaches begin to investigate the three fundamental elements of the resolution: actor, object, and act. To understand how these elements fit into the development of an Affirmative plan, consider the resolution:

> Resolved: The United States Federal Government should increase its constructive engagement with the governments of one or more of the following countries: Afghanistan, Iran, Lebanon, the Palestinian Authority, and Syria, and it should include offering them a security guarantee(s) and/or a substantial increase in foreign assistance.

Who is the actor? This resolution indicates that the United States Federal Government should enact a plan—but the federal government has three branches: legislative, judicial, and executive. Therefore, Affirmative teams must decide whether the actor is the entire federal government or a specific branch. They make this decision by researching how the three branches can and cannot increase constructive engagement with the list of nations provided in the resolution. Choosing to specify a branch of government allows the Affirmative team to make detailed arguments about their agent, but will also allow the Negative team to argue that a different agent could better implement the plan.

Who or what is the object of the resolution? In the resolution above, the object is the nations listed—Afghanistan, Iran, Lebanon, the Palestinian Authority, and Syria. The Affirmative is limited to debating only about those countries. While they may choose to meet the resolution by selecting one or any combination of nations, the Affirmative may not add a nation to this list.

A plan that addressed Iran, Lebanon, and Iraq would be "extra-topical" because Iraq was not included in the resolution.

How is the act qualified? Every debate resolution indicates how debaters should qualify the plan's action. In the example resolution, the Affirmative must create a plan that includes the terms "increase," "constructive engagement," "offering," or "substantial increase." Debaters define these vague terms using government documents and policy briefs that often include specific definitions from past government policies. For example, an Affirmative team might use evidence that defined "constructive engagement" in prior Middle East policymaking or that defines what it means for the United States to "offer" a security guarantee. Many resolutions include the term "significantly" or "substantial." In these cases, debaters look for evidence that indicates how past policymakers have quantified the size of their action, usually by percentage of increase. Once a team has defined the qualified terms, they must carefully check that all of their evidence uses the same definitions. For example, if the team has defined constructive engagement as sending food aid, they must make sure their evidence defines constructive engagement to mean food aid and not sending tanks.

Topicality from the Negative Perspective

Negative teams use topicality in two ways. First, topicality is a voting issue that protects Negative teams from having to debate unpredictable cases. Second, the Negative can use topicality to make the Affirmative clarify portions of their plan. These clarifications can then be cross-applied to strengthen the Negative arguments made elsewhere in the debate.

ARGUING AGAINST UNPREDICTABLE CASES

Some Affirmative teams attempt to win the round by presenting an unpredictable case and expecting the Negative to be unprepared for the debate. The Negative team's best response is that such plan is not topical and the debate is therefore unfair. They will present this topicality violation in the 1NC. The Negative may also present other types of arguments but frame them in terms of trying to argue against an unpredictable case. Using this strategy, the Negative includes topicality in each of its arguments. All of these arguments will include the caveat: the Negative arguments are terrible, but that is because the Affirmative presented an unpredictable case.

For example, let's suppose the year's resolution is "Resolved: The United States Federal Government should substantially increase its democracy assistance for one or more of the following: Bahrain, Egypt, Libya, Syria, Tunisia, Yemen." The Affirmative presents a plan calling for increased democracy assistance for Iraq. The Negative responds with a topicality argument accusing the Affirmative of being unpredictable and non-topical because Iraq was not listed in the resolution. In this round, the Negative is not arguing that the Iraqi Affirmative is a bad idea. Rather, they are arguing that the debate is unfair because the Negative preparations were for a debate about Bahrain, Egypt, Libya, Syria, Tunisia, and Yemen, not Iraq.

USING TOPICALITY TO SUPPORT OTHER ARGUMENTS

The Negative team may use topicality violations even when they are prepared to debate the Affirmative plan. In these rounds, the topicality violation becomes one of many tools of the Negative team. This strategy takes three common forms. First, by analyzing the Affirmative's responses to a topicality violation, the Negative might be able to turn one or more of the Affirmative's arguments against them. Second, even though the Negative has specific or generic arguments, they may also have a strong topicality argument and beat the Affirmative in a definitional debate. Finally, the Negative team might present their topicality argument in order to win a disadvantage. This last strategy begins when the Negative claims that the Affirmative plan violates the quantifiable term of the resolution, such as "significantly increase." For example, if an Affirmative plan increases funding by 10 percent, the Negative topicality violation might argue that anything less than 15 percent is not a significant increase. The Affirmative responds by presenting evidence that the plan does constitute a significant increase. The Negative then cross-applies that evidence to their disadvantage scenario, which argues that a significant increase will cause the impact to occur. The Affirmative's own evidence becomes the disadvantage's link. This strategy is common with Negative teams who have a disadvantage that links to a generic action in the resolution, e.g., significantly increasing funding but not having a specific link for the Affirmative plan.

Writing a Topicality Argument

The 1NC introduces a topicality argument using the following structure:

1. Definition

2. Violation

3. Standards

4. Voter

Maintaining this structure might seem unimaginative, but a common structure allows the judge to focus her attention on the quality of your analysis and arguments rather than trying to understand a new speech structure.

SHELLS

The shell contains all of the components of the argument that the 1NC should present except for the Affirmative's specific violation. This information is added after the Negative team has seen the text of the Affirmative plan. Having the basic elements of their topicality argument prepared before the round enables the Negative to listen closely during the 1AC for any small changes that the Affirmative team may have made since the two teams last debated each other.

To understand how each portion of a topicality violation functions, consider the resolution:

> Resolved: That the United States Federal Government should substantially reduce its agricultural support, at least eliminating nearly all of the domestic subsidies, for biofuels, concentrated animal feeding operations, corn, cotton, dairy, fisheries, rice, soybeans, sugar and/or wheat.

And the Affirmative plan text: "The United States Federal Government should reduce its agricultural support by reducing all domestic sugar subsidies by twenty percent."

DEFINITION

Topicality definitions should be short and easily understood. A good definition is a direct quote from a dictionary, a government policy document, or a legal document that authoritatively defines a term in the resolution. This quotation should be structured like any other piece of evidence and must include both a tag and full citation.

When selecting a definition, debate teams try to be as specific as possible. For example, when debating the resolution above, debaters used definitions from agriculture industry publications rather than from general dictionaries. What is the difference between these definitions? A common topicality argument deals with the term "substantially." A general dictionary might define "substantially" as "to a significant extent." A definition from an agricultural publication might define a substantial change in funding as a net increase or decrease equal to at least 25 percent of all currently appropriated funds. This definition is better then the dictionary definition because it clarifies "substantially" in terms of the specific topic.

VIOLATION

The topicality violation is a simple, one-sentence explanation of why the Affirmative has not met the Negative's definition. For example, "The Affirmative Plan does not decrease agricultural subsidies by at least 25 percent of all currently appropriated funds."

STANDARDS

Standards present the judge with specific criteria for evaluating if and why a definition creates a good debate. The following is a list of definitional standards, the questions they ask, and how each standard would be used in a debate on the above resolution. None of the standards is superior to the others; each is used as the debaters see fit in the round.

Breadth vs. depth is a standard used to determine if a definition encourages debaters to know a small amount about a variety of arguments (breadth) or a good deal about a very small set of arguments (depth). Definitions that provide a broad interpretation of the resolution run the risk of expanding the topic to the point that it becomes unmanageable. A definition that allows the Affirmative to reduce agricultural subsides by reducing the number of potential subsidies rather than reducing actually distributed subsidies might be topical, but it functionally doubles the size of the resolution.

Brightline asks if the definition clearly separates what is and is not topical. Some definitions only indicate what a word means and do not clarify what a word does not mean. For example, a definition of "substantial" says that the word means "25 percent," then it does not definitively create a brightline. A definition that says substantial means "no less than a 25 percent change" creates clear brightline by explaining what is and is not substantial.

Education asks if the definition encourages an educational debate. Given that any conversation could be educational, the best debaters focus on whether the definition facilitates topic-based education. Even if a definition is logically sound and provides ample ground to both sides of the debate, if it is not the standard used by policymakers, it is arguably noneducational. For example, in the subsidies debate above, a definition from *Agricultural Weekly* is more educational than one from mass media sources such as *Time* magazine.

Effects topicality asks if the Affirmative plan meets the resolution only after taking a number of steps. Most judges believe that the Affirmative plan must be the immediate implementation of a topical policy. Any plan that requires more than one action to be topical is considered unfair. For example, an Affirmative team could offer a plan to increase funding for NASA, arguing that the plan will require the government to decrease agricultural subsidies as a result. In this example, the Negative team could respond with an "effects topicality" violation, arguing that the subsequent effects of the plan and not the plan itself are topical.

Framer's intent asks if the debaters are interpreting the resolution in the way intended by the topic committee. Since the topic committee spends considerable time determining the most fair and educational resolution, debaters and judges generally seek to adhere to the committee's intent.

Division of ground asks if the proposed definition is fair to both the Affirmative and Negative. This standard is judged by the amount of literature available in support of both the Affirmative and Negative positions that uses or adheres to the definition.

Real world asks if the definition is one that a policymaker would use. Real-world interpretations are found in academic and government documents pertaining to the resolution. For example, a definition from a Department of Agriculture publication is real world.

VOTERS

Topicality arguments conclude with reasons why the judge should vote on topicality before addressing any other arguments in the round. Most judges automatically evaluate topicality before judging other arguments. But some judges will not do so unless they are persuaded by a clear reason to vote on topicality. The two most common voters are "fairness" and "education." Fairness argues that the judge cannot vote for an Affirmative team who has created an unbalanced debate that the Negative was not prepared for. Education argues that the primary goal of debate is to educate debaters, and the best education occurs when both teams debate the same resolution.

Affirmative Answers to Topicality Arguments

Affirmative teams should critically analyze their plan text to determine what topicality violations they might encounter. They can prepare basic answers to those arguments and then fill in any necessary details during the round. Occasionally the 2AC may have to respond to an unanticipated topicality argument, but with a few adjustments, she can usually combine several pre-developed arguments to present a compelling speech.

Affirmative prepared answers to topicality violations should include the following arguments:

1. **We meet:** The Affirmative team argues that they meet the Negative's definitions.
2. **Counter-definition:** The Affirmative argues that, in addition to meeting the Negative definition, they have a better definition.
3. **Reasons to prefer the Affirmative's definition:** The Affirmative argues that the Affirmative's new definition is better than the Negative's for a number of reasons. For example, it clearly divides Affirmative and Negative ground.
4. **Affirmative standards:** The Affirmative answers each of the Negative standards with their own reasons why the Affirmative plan is topical and why their standards are best for debate. In addition to refuting the Negative standards, the Affirmative should make two additional arguments.
   a. Literature checks abuse—the debate is fair because other authors have already used this definition.
   b. Clash checks abuse—if both teams can make good arguments, the judge has no reason to vote on topicality.
5. **Voters:** The Affirmative responds to the Negative's voting arguments by claiming that because both teams were able to

make arguments about the resolution, abuse has not occurred and topicality is not a voting issue.

The Affirmative may also make a voting argument called a "time skew." This term is used to label an opponent's argument as an attempt to waste time in the debate rather than make substantive arguments. A topicality time skew occurs when the Negative team presents several short, poorly developed topicality violations and several well-developed case-specific arguments. The Negative team uses this strategy to prevent the Affirmative from adequately answering the case arguments.

The Affirmative should respond to time skews by arguing that because the Negative team has provided case-specific arguments, the Affirmative plan was predictable and the Negative could have engaged in policy-specific debate. This response consists of both defensive and offensive arguments. Defensively, the Affirmative accuses the Negative team of sacrificing education in favor of strategy. Offensively, the Affirmative asks the judge to punish the Negative team by voting Affirmative, thus discouraging a strategy that prevents educational debate on the topic area.

Topicality Arguments Throughout the Debate Round

Topicality arguments are presented in the 1NC and responded to in the 2AC. The 2AC must make a strategic decision about the amount of time to spend on topicality and the type of arguments to make. Some 2ACs make both offensive and defensive arguments against topicality, ensuring a win for the Affirmative team in that argument. While this is the strongest strategy, it takes time away from answering other arguments. In some rounds, the 2AC will only make defensive arguments, either because doing so takes less time or because she wants to encourage the Negative team to drop topicality in the 2NC. Based on the 2AC's answers, the Negative team must then determine if they want to pursue these arguments during the Negative block (the 2NC and 1NR).

Dropping Topicality

Negative teams should drop topicality if the 2AC has made an overwhelming variety of arguments against a topicality violation while under-covering another Negative argument. If the 2AC has not made any offensive arguments against the topicality argument, the Negative team can drop topicality by simply not including the argument in the 2NC or 1NR roadmap. However, if the 2AC made offensive arguments, the Negative team must answer those before dropping topicality. For example, the 2AC made a time skew argument maintaining that the Negative team was only using topicality to prevent her from providing better answers to a disadvantage. The 2NC must respond to this argument by explaining why the 1NC topicality argument was necessary to clarify a specific part of the Affirmative plan. Once this strategy is explained, the 2NC can move on to a different argument. This signifies to the judge and the Affirmative team that the Negative team has dropped topicality.

Going for Topicality

Negative teams win topicality by proving that the Affirmative team has been abusive *and* that the abuse requires the judge to vote on topicality before any other argument. For this strategy to succeed, the 2NR should spend considerable time on topicality, explaining his argument and reminding the judge of the abuse that occurred in the round. The remainder of the time should be devoted to making one or two solid arguments (such as a disadvantage) that could both win the round and demonstrate the abuse caused by the Affirmative. Because topicality is a prima facie voting issue, the Negative only need win topicality to win the round.

Interpreting and Specifying the Affirmative Plan

At times, an Affirmative plan text might appear topical, but the Negative cannot be certain because they are unsure what the plan does. When facing an unclear plan, the Negative can present a specification or "spec" argument that presses the Affirmative team to clarify how their plan will be enacted. Topicality and specification arguments are often confused with each other because they use similar standards and voters. However, the content of these arguments is very different. Whereas topicality arguments force the Affirmative to specify how their plan falls within the resolution, spec arguments claim that the Affirmative has not presented a clear proposal, thus making the debate vague and unfair.

Negative teams have two reasons for using specification violations. Either they are confused about how the Affirmative will work, or they are attempting to use the Affirmative's answers to support Negative arguments made elsewhere in the debate. Consider an Affirmative plan for the resolution:

> Resolved: The United States Federal Government should substantially reduce the size of its nuclear weapons arsenal and/or substantially reduce and restrict the role and/or missions of its nuclear weapons arsenal.

Plan: The United States Federal Government should dismantle its nuclear Trident warhead arsenal.

The Negative team could ask a number of questions about this plan during cross-examination. These questions might include: Who will enforce the dismantling? Who will dismantle the weapons? What does dismantling a weapon mean? Where will the dismantled weapon parts go? Asking these questions is acceptable but takes away from time to investigate other arguments. Framing these same questions as a 1NC specification violation gains the same answers, but strategically uses the Affirmative speech time rather than the Negative's cross-examination time.

The Negative presents specification violations in the 1NC, using the same organization and standards as a topicality violation. The only difference is that specification arguments make a demand for more information rather than arguing that the Affirmative has violated a definition. The two types of specification arguments are: agent and implementation. Both are argued as prima facie reasons to reject the Affirmative.

Agent specification (A-spec) argues that the Affirmative has failed to specify *who* will execute the plan. The United States Federal Government has three branches and multiple agencies. Failure to specify which government office will implement the plan prevents the Negative from presenting specific arguments against the particular government agency's ability to solve the harms.

Implementation specification (I-spec) argues that the plan text has failed to specify *how* the plan is to be implemented or enforced. Failure to specify implementation makes it difficult for the Negative to argue that the implementation will not work or to prove that other methods of implementation would work better.

Answering Specification Violations

The Affirmative answers specification violations by simultaneously providing the information demanded by the violation and arguing that that information is not important enough to justify presenting a violation or voting against the Affirmative team.

The Affirmative team begins making these answers during the cross-examination of the 1NC. The Affirmative asks the 1NC speaker what arguments they have been prevented from making because of the Affirmative's (presumed) lack of specification. The Negative will respond in one of two ways. First, they might provide a generic list of arguments. That list might not prove any abuse occurred, however. In that case, the 2AC will spend minimal time answering the violation. She need only prove that no abuse has occurred in the round.

Alternately, the Negative could point out a specific argument that they could not make because of the Affirmative's violation. When this occurs, the 2AC should first provide any information demanded by the violation. Then, she should argue that, while not being able to present a particular argument may have annoyed the Negative, it does not prove that the Affirmative case is abusive.

Although topicality and specification theory arguments address different aspects of the Affirmative plan, they work toward the same goal, creating a fair and educational debate round. Topicality and specification arguments are the most common arguments in debate, occurring in novice rounds and the final rounds of national tournaments.

KEY CONCEPTS

1. Topicality Affirmatives must engage the actor, object, and mechanism stated in the resolution.

2. Negative teams can present a topicality argument when they believe the Affirmative has violated the resolution or to force the Affirmative to spend time proving that the judge can legitimately vote for the Affirmative plan.

3. Topicality violations are presented in a standard format and include a definition, violation, standard, and voters.

4. Topicality and specification arguments are prima facie voter issues. The judge can vote against a team based on these arguments before evaluating any of the other arguments in the round.

14

DISADVANTAGES

Disadvantages (also known as disads or DAs) are policy-based arguments that create a basis to justify rejecting the Affirmative plan. This chapter begins by introducing disadvantages and explaining why a Negative team would use them. Next, we look at disadvantages from the Affirmative side, highlighting critical elements of the argument the Affirmative must answer and explaining how a crafty Affirmative team can turn a disadvantage into an advantage.

Disadvantage Basics

Negative teams use disadvantages to explain how the Affirmative case, despite its good intentions, will actually increase suffering, economic hardship, or environmental destruction. Negative teams win rounds with disadvantages by proving that a disadvantage of the Affirmative plan outweighs the Affirmative's advantages. To win the round, many Negative teams will argue that the Affirmative will result in nuclear war, genocide and/or extinction. Novice debaters are usually shocked by this approach. How could an Affirmative case that attempts to save children from hunger result in a nuclear war? Tying even the most philanthropic Affirmative plan to threats of extinction requires the Negative to carefully craft a story that ties together the work of multiple authors, gradually inflating the consequences of the plan to magnificent proportions.

To create a viable disadvantage scenario, the Negative must present the following components, each consisting of a tag, citation, and piece of evidence. Components that are bolded are essential to any disadvantage; the other elements are an optional means of presenting a more nuanced scenario.

> **Uniqueness:** Provides information on the present state of affairs indicating that no problem exists in the status quo.
>
> **Brink:** Sometimes contained within the same evidence as uniqueness, the brink indicates that the disadvantage scenario is on the verge of happening and that a small action will cause major change.
>
> **Link:** Shows how and why the Affirmative case relates to the disadvantage scenario, indicating that the plan will alter the present course of events.
> *Internal link*—an additional piece of evidence sometimes used to tie the link to the impact.
>
> **Impact:** Illustrates the terrible event the Affirmative plan will cause. This element is analogous to Affirmative harms.

To understand how a disadvantage is constructed and argued, let's examine an economy disadvantage. This is a common argument used to prove that the Affirmative plan directly or indirectly disrupts the American economy.

EXAMPLE OF AN ECONOMY DISADVANTAGE

The most basic economy disadvantage argues that the Affirmative policy will directly disrupt the otherwise stable U.S. economy and that this disruption will have adverse effects on society. The Negative argues that the Affirmative case causes the disadvantage by spending money that has already been allocated for a different project or simply does not exist. Then, the Negative team presents evidence that additional spending would upset the balance of trade, which is critical to a healthy U.S. economy. If the Negative wanted to extend this argument, they could assert that because the U.S. economy affects the global economy, destabilizing it could lead to the collapse of the world economy, which, in turn, increases the chances of war. The Negative team introduces this argument in the 1NC or 2NC by presenting uniqueness, link, and impact evidence.

> **Uniqueness:** Evidence will prove that the economy is not currently in danger of collapsing.
>
> **Link:** Evidence will argue that the Affirmative plan directly disrupts the economy by spending money to implement the plan.
>
> **Impact:** Evidence will show that the negative outcomes of the plan are greater than the benefits of the Affirmative solvency or advantages. Because the disadvantage must outweigh the Affirmative plan, the Negative team will select the largest

implication they can find, such as nuclear war, extinction, economic collapse, or genocide.

As we have learned, uniqueness, link, and impact are the three essential aspects of any disadvantage that the 1NC must present. If the Affirmative challenges the Negative's scenario, the Negative will present two other parts of a disadvantage: brink and internal link.

BRINK

Brink evidence attempts to prove that the link or impact is on the verge of happening in the status quo. For the economy disadvantage, a brink argument would state that even though the economy is currently stable, it is also extremely delicate and a single shift in policy would cause it to destabilize. Good uniqueness evidence will often make this type of argument, but sometimes the Negative must independently prove that the disadvantage impact scenario is on the verge of occurring. Brink arguments make the threat of the disadvantage more immediate, but can also make the impact scenario appear inevitable.

INTERNAL LINK

Internal links unite uniqueness, link, and impact evidence into a coherent narrative. In the example above, finding evidence that an Affirmative plan will lead to complete economic collapse would be difficult. Since no qualified author would make a case for complete economic collapse based on a single policy initiative, linking the Affirmative to the disadvantage impact can take several steps, or internal links. For example, if the Negative presented evidence that the Affirmative plan would hurt manufacturing, they would need internal-link evidence stating that strong manufacturing is necessary to prevent economic collapse. After presenting those two pieces of evidence, the 1NC would present an economic collapse impact.

The quality of the internal links is directly related to the plausibility of the scenario. Disadvantages with fewer internal links are more likely to withstand Affirmative criticism since chaining together longer scenarios makes a disadvantage appear unlikely and convoluted. When in doubt, offer internal-link evidence only if it is absolutely necessary to the disadvantage.

Negatives argue economy disadvantages every year because Affirmative plans always require funding or have a spillover effect on the economy. Additionally, diverting money from one program to another always has political implications. Other perennial disadvantages include political scenarios, election scenarios, state vs. federal rights, and business confidence. To understand the similarities and differences between disadvantages, examine the following example, a politics disadvantage.

Politics Disadvantage

Politics disadvantages argue that the Affirmative plan will have negative repercussions on other polices being debated in Congress. How and why this might happen depends on the disadvantage scenario. For instance, some politics disadvantages will claim that asking Congress to consider the plan means it won't be able to focus on another policy of greater importance. Other scenarios assert that adopting the plan will anger certain policymakers, who will retaliate by blocking passage of a different important policy.

To better understand a politics disadvantage, assume that the Affirmative has presented the plan: "The United States Federal Government should place a trade embargo on China." The politics disadvantage argues that adopting the plan will distract from the current political agenda, which is focused on lowering gas prices. The components of the disadvantage might be:

Uniqueness: Congress is focused on lowering gas prices now—adding anything to its agenda could derail that initiative.

Brink: Lowering gas prices now is critical—failing to act will destroy any chance of lowering prices for years to come.

Link: Altering our foreign policy toward China is extremely controversial and would involve Congress in a protracted debate. Acting now will change Congress's agenda and prevent passage of the gas legislation.

Impact 1: Rising gas prices will collapse the economy.

Impact 2: Economic decline causes nuclear and biological war.

Political and economic disadvantages are nothing more than combinations of warranted claims used either to argue that a scenario is feasible or to draw a scenario out to its logical conclusions. Beyond working to clarify a destructive effect of the Affirmative plan, disadvantages can vary wildly both in scenario and organization. Debaters will typically prefer a piece of evidence that includes multiple aspects of the disadvantage. Although rare, disadvantages will sometimes have only a single piece of evidence that includes both the uniqueness and link—these indicate the special relationship between the plan and the disadvantage scenario. Determining how a scenario fits together is essential to the creation of a disadvantage scenario. Examining past disadvantages is the best way of learning the process.

Answering a Disadvantage

The Affirmative must convince the judge that the combined impacts of the disadvantages do not outweigh the positive outcomes of their plan. To do so, the Affirmative will use a combination of evidence comparison, analytical arguments, and impact assessment. These arguments can be classified into three categories: uniqueness arguments, "takeout" arguments that address the Negative's logic, and "turns," which argue that the Negative's arguments actually support the Affirmative plan.

UNIQUENESS

Uniqueness arguments question the current status of the disadvantage scenario. Since disadvantage scenarios are based on real-world controversies, the Affirmative can usually use a wide variety of authors and make a range of claims to challenge the Negative scenario. Uniqueness arguments are defensive; they mitigate the disadvantage rather than turn it into an advantage for the Affirmative. The most common types of uniqueness arguments are:

Non-unique: Non-unique claims point out that given the status quo, the disadvantage scenario will occur independently of the passage of the Affirmative's plan—in other words, the Affirmative plan is not the sole reason that problems arise. For example, if the disadvantage says "New environmental regulations will pass now," the Affirmative would contend that "environmental regulations will inevitably fail to pass." Since nonunique arguments can completely mitigate a disadvantage, both the Affirmative and Negative should spend considerable time in the rebuttals analyzing the warrants and author qualifications of competing uniqueness and non-unique arguments.

Uniqueness overwhelms the link: This argument states that the disadvantage scenario does not have a brink. This means that even if the plan links to the disadvantage, the plan does not affect the scenario enough to cause the impact to occur. For example, consider a disadvantage with uniqueness, "President Obama's agenda has full support in Congress—there is no threat of filibuster or blockage" and the link "Increasing foreign aid to the Middle East (the Affirmative plan) will destabilize President Obama's agenda." In this example, the uniqueness evidence overwhelms the threat posed by the Affirmative plan because it demonstrates that no one would be angry enough about the plan to stop Obama's agenda. Arguing that uniqueness overwhelms the link is a good strategy if the Negative has over-stated their uniqueness, making the rest of their disadvantage unlikely to occur. This is a common mistake made by Negative teams that have not considered how their various pieces of evidence work together.

Takeouts

Takeouts are defensive arguments designed to identify the logical holes in the disadvantage. They question the connections between the uniqueness, links, internal links, and impacts. The most common takeout arguments are:

No link: No link arguments claim that the Negative scenario is not related to the plan. This type of argument can be made analytically but is stronger when supported by evidence. For example, the Negative has presented link evidence that the plan will disrupt the economy. The Affirmative could respond with an analytical argument that investigates the claims in the Negative's evidence, or the Affirmative could present a superior piece of evidence arguing that the plan will not affect the economy.

No internal link: No internal link arguments claim that a link between the plan and the disadvantage doesn't matter because that link will not result in the disadvantage impact. No internal link arguments are common when the Negative team has presented a very short disadvantage. For example, consider the link "plan will destabilize the economy" and the impact "economic depression will cause nuclear war." There is a large chasm between destabilizing the economy and a nuclear war. The Affirmative team should respond to this faulty disadvantage with an analytical argument stating that destabilizing the economy does not necessarily lead to an economic depression and that the economy has been destabilized many times without nuclear war resulting.

No impact: No impact arguments are designed to diminish or negate the magnitude of a disadvantage impact. These arguments prove that the impacts are implausible, insignificant, or exaggerated. They may also challenge the importance of the impacts by questioning the disadvantage timeframe. For example, the Negative team has presented an economy disadvantage that claims an economic decline will lead to war. The 2AC could present a no impact argument showing that no evidence exists that nations will attack one another simply because their economies are in trouble. This argument can be presented with analytics referencing previous economic hardships that have not resulted in war or through evidentiary claims made by economists that an economic downturn will not result in war.

Turns

Turns are offensive claims the Affirmative utilizes to make the disadvantage into an Affirmative advantage. The Affirmative can turn a disadvantage in a number of ways; the most common are link turns and impact turns.

Link turns: Link turns argue that the plan will prevent the impact from occurring. For example, the Negative disadvantage says that Congress must balance the budget now and the plan prevents it from doing so. The link turn would be made from evidence to argue that the Affirmative's plan is *critical* to balancing the budget.

Impact turns: Impact turns argue that the disadvantage impact scenario is actually an advantage for the Affirmative. For example, the disadvantage says that the plan causes global warming and global warming causes extinction of a specific species of fish. An impact turn would say that global warming is essential to preventing extinction of the same species of fish. Impact turns must be made with evidence, and that evidence must be either more recent or make more logical claims than the Negative's impact evidence. Additionally, an impact turn requires that the Affirmative team concede the rest of the disadvantage. For example, the disadvantage claims the plan will prevent Congress from passing legislation that is critical to balancing the federal budget. The Affirmative can concede that they stop the measure from passing, but their impact turn would argue that balancing the budget is bad because it would require cutting critical programs. If the Affirmative's evidence and arguments are strong enough, the impact turn will allow the Affirmative to claim the disadvantage as a new advantage to their plan. However, if the Negative's evidence and arguments are stronger, then they will win the disadvantage because the Affirmative has not challenged the uniqueness and has conceded the link.

When presenting turn arguments, Affirmative teams must be careful not to "double-turn" themselves. Think of a double-turn in this way: if you are driving a car and make a U-turn, then you are facing the opposite direction, but if you make another U-turn, you end up facing the original direction again (a double-turn). Not only does a double-turn waste your time, it also strengthens your opponent's argument. In debate, you may make a link turn *or* an impact turn. A double-turn occurs when the Affirmative turns both the link and the impact of a disadvantage scenario. For example, see if you can determine the problem with the Affirmative answers to an economics disadvantage.

> Original Negative disadvantage:
>> Link: Plan prevents Obama's reelection
>>
>> Impact: Romney presidency increases risk of terrorism
>
> Affirmative answers:
>> Link Turn: Plan ensures Obama's reelection
>>
>> Impact Turn: Obama's reelection is more likely to spur terrorist attacks against the United States

In this example, the Affirmative eliminates a disadvantage against their case with a link turn. However, they also present an argument against the Affirmative plan with the impact turn. Unfortunately, this strategy is flawed because it has created a new impact scenario against the Affirmative. Rather than the plan leading to terrorism because of a Romney presidency, the Affirmative has now argued that their plan increases terrorism because of an Obama presidency. If this happens, an attentive Negative team will label the impact turn as a double-turn. The Negative will then assert that the Affirmative cannot argue against the disadvantage scenario since so doing undermines the Affirmative's claims. Double-turns might seem like an easy problem to avoid, but they are surprisingly common, even in varsity debates. This confusion usually occurs when debaters are rushed before giving a speech or team partners have not conferred about their strategy.

Affirmative Impact Assessment

Regardless of how the Affirmative answers a disadvantage, they must always provide an impact assessment. This involves comparing the impact scenario of the disadvantage to the Affirmative advantages by weighing the probability, timeframe, and magnitude of the Affirmative and Negative impacts. Then the Affirmative clarifies why they have won even if both the Affirmative and Negative impacts occur. This strategy is known as arguing that the "case outweighs the disadvantage." For example, the disadvantage claims that the plan causes regional conflict and the Affirmative advantage claims to solve global war. In this round, the Affirmative's impact (global war) outweighs the disadvantage impact (regional war).

Creating a 2AC Disadvantage Block

The 2AC attacks a disadvantage using a "block"—an assortment of analytical and evidentiary arguments. The goal of the 2AC block is to answer the disadvantage by presenting a wide variety of arguments. This strategy is designed to force the Negative team to either drop the disadvantage or to spend so much time answering the 2AC block that they under-cover another argument.

2AC blocks for common disadvantages such as economic and political scenarios should be created before the tournament. These prepared answers extend specific pieces of evidence from the 1AC and present new evidence and analytical arguments to answer a disadvantage. The best 2AC blocks mix several types of arguments and never present two of the same type in a row. For example, a poor 2AC block might present three evidentiary non-unique answers followed by two analytical no links. This is a poor organizational strategy because the 2NC can quickly "group" together all of the non-unique evidence and answer with one or two arguments. Consider the time trade-off for this strategy: the Negative responds much more quickly than the Affirmative.

A superior 2AC block would vary these arguments; for example, by reading an evidentiary non-unique, an analytical no link, followed by an analytical non-unique argument, an evidentiary no link, and an evidentiary non-unique, the 2AC still has presented five arguments—three supported by evidence and two supported by analytics. For the Affirmative, this block takes the same amount of time to present as the previous example. However, this organization will take much more time for the Negative to answer. Yes, the Negative could still group together all of the non-unique and no link answers, but this will require the Negative to gloss over the differences between the evidentiary and analytical arguments. Additionally, grouping the arguments, rather than answering them line by line, appears as a weak strategy on the flow. If the Negative wants to win the disadvantage, she will have to answer each of the 2AC arguments separately and take much more time.

How to Concede a Disadvantage When Negative

Okay, you've made a mistake. The disadvantage that you thought would be a game changer has done you no good. In fairness, the 2AC was damn impressive. So what should you do? First, never ignore an argument and hope it will go away. After speaking with your partner, you may decide to abandon the disadvantage. In debate jargon, this is known as "kicking" the disadvantage. How do you determine whether you should kick on the disadvantage?

DID THE AFFIRMATIVE MAKE OFFENSIVE AND DEFENSIVE ARGUMENTS AGAINST THE DISADVANTAGE?

The Affirmative can use offensive arguments such as turns even after the Negative drops the disadvantage. To avoid this situation, the Negative should selectively concede the Affirmative's defensive arguments. Since most defensive arguments claim that the Negative's scenario is not possible, conceding these claims renders the Affirmative's offensive claims inconsequential because the disadvantage scenario will not occur.

For example, assume that the Negative team offered an economy disadvantage that claimed the Affirmative plan would result in economic decline. The 2AC made two responses:

1. Non-unique: Policies similar to the plan already exist, so there's no reason why adopting our policy would uniquely cause the economy to collapse.

2. Impact turn: Passing the plan will cause the disadvantage to happen, spurring economic decline in the short term. However this decline will have a net beneficial outcome for the world population. Economic decline now prevents a worse economic decline in the future.

To kick this economy disadvantage, the Negative should concede the Affirmative's non-unique (policies similar to the plan already exist). This concession takes out the impact turn by arguing that the disadvantage scenario is inevitable in the status quo. By making this concession, the Negative is able to kick the disadvantage.

DID THE AFFIRMATIVE READ ONLY OFFENSE ON THE DISADVANTAGE?

The Negative team must answer all of the Affirmative's turns before dropping the disadvantage. If the Affirmative has provided superior evidence showing that the disadvantage scenario is actually an advantage to their plan, then the Negative team should concede those turns and focus attention on winning a stronger argument with a larger impact. However, if the turned disadvantage is the largest impact in the round, the Negative needs to dedicate its time to disproving the turn.

To disprove the turn, the Negative should focus on how the turn relates to the other Affirmative arguments. Affirmative teams typically present as much evidence as possible in support of the turn and forget to clarify how the turn and impact of the disadvantage compare with the other impacts in the round. Put another way, the Affirmative relies too heavily on claims from evidence and fails to make comparative claims backed by analytical arguments. A good Negative team will counter this strategy by focusing on just a few arguments and providing superior impact analysis. When a disadvantage debate comes down to comparing turns versus original Negative arguments, judges tend to vote for whoever has made the best analysis of competing claims.

When analyzing disadvantages, judges compare the probability, timeframe, and magnitude of the impact to that of the Affirmative advantages. Explaining why the ramifications of the disadvantage are bigger, quicker, and deadlier than the scenarios solved by the plan is critical to winning the debate. Many judges will read the evidence from the disadvantage to resolve these questions, so directing them to review your strongest cards is extremely important.

KEY CONCEPTS

1. The disadvantage is an argument presented in the 1NC or 2NC that focuses on the damages caused by enacting the plan.

2. Disadvantages must include uniqueness, link, and an impact. They may also include a brink and an internal link.

3. The 2AC should respond to the disadvantage with a variety of arguments, including reasons why the disadvantage would not happen and why implementing the plan would actually alleviate the problems the Negative presented.

4. To win a disadvantage, the Negative team must win two arguments: that the Affirmative action prevents a better policy from being implemented and that the impact of the disadvantage outweighs the advantages of the Affirmative.

5. Avoid double-turns and take advantage of any double-turns your opponent makes.

15
COUNTERPLANS

Counterplans (CP) are rival proposals to the Affirmative plan. This chapter will discuss their structure and explain why and how the Negative creates and uses a counterplan argument. Then, we address Affirmative answers to counterplans and the theoretical arguments commonly used to determine which counterplans are fair to both teams. Finally, this chapter explains how judges evaluate counterplans.

Counterplan Basics

Negatives use counterplans when they want to advocate a position other than the status quo. These debaters agree that the status quo is flawed, but think that alternative policy options, often outside the scope of the resolution, could solve the Affirmative harms.

Counterplans are presented in the same manner as Affirmative plans. They have a written plan text presented in the 1NC that cannot be changed after it has been presented. While the debate community has no formal standard for what constitutes a fair counterplan, most debaters agree that counterplans are fair when they ensure a division of ground determined by two criteria. First, they must be non-topical; they must solve the problems the 1AC presented without defending the resolution. Second, and perhaps more important, the Negative must demonstrate competitiveness. They must offer some reason why the Affirmative plan and the Negative counterplan are mutually exclusive and cannot be enacted at the same time. Proving competitiveness is easiest when using evidence that explicitly presents the plan and counterplan as options that cannot coexist. Unfortunately, this evidence is very difficult to find. Consequently, Negatives generally prove competitiveness through a net benefit, indicating that adopting the counterplan is better than implementing both the counterplan and the plan. Net benefits often include a disadvantage linked to the plan but not the counterplan.

Creating a Negative Counterplan

Counterplans are held to the same standards as Affirmative plans. Just like the plan, they must meet each of the stock issues (inherency, harms, topicality, significance, and solvency) and contain a text advocating a policy initiative. To save time, 1NC may cross-apply inherency, harms, significance, and solvency evidence from the Affirmative case. However, the 1NC may present a piece of evidence supporting the counterplan's inherency, harms, significance, or solvency if the Negative's evidence is better or very different from the Affirmative's. Then, the 1NC presents a counterplan text as well as solvency evidence specific to the counterplan. The net benefit for the counterplan may be presented after its solvency just as an Affirmative team would present an advantage. Or, the net benefit might be presented as an additional off-case argument—a disadvantage, for example.

INHERENCY

Just like the Affirmative plan, the Negative must prove that their policy has not already been implemented. They usually do this by cross-applying the Affirmative's inherency or presenting a new, short piece of evidence.

COUNTERPLAN TEXT

Most counterplans will have a text that is very similar to the Affirmative plan. For example, if the Affirmative plan states, "The United States Federal Government should recognize the Palestinian Authority," the counterplan might read, "The United States Federal Government should recognize the Palestinian Authority on the condition that Hamas withdraw all military forces from Gaza." By either adding or removing something from the Affirmative plan text, the counterplan asks the judge to evaluate two similar polices.

SOLVENCY

The Negative typically presents new evidence that the counterplan can solve the harms outlined by the Affirmative. However, if the plan and counterplan are very similar, the Negative might be able to save time by cross-applying the Affirmative's solvency evidence.

NET BENEFIT

Net benefits are similar to Affirmative advantages because they give an external reason why the counterplan is better than the status quo. However, the Negative has the extra burden of also proving that the counterplan is better than the Affirmative plan. The Negative can present the net benefit either through a disadvantage or through solvency.

Disadvantage net benefits function as a two-pronged attack: the Negative can use the disadvantage as a stand-alone, round-winning argument or as a net benefit for the counterplan. Using the disadvantage as a net benefit forces the Affirmative team to spend a lot more time answering the counterplan and the disadvantage because the Affirmative runs the risk of losing to either the counterplan *or* the disadvantage. For example, if the Affirmative plan presents a policy that is to be implemented through legislation, the Negative could present a counterplan stating that the policy be enacted by Executive Order. The net benefit would be a disadvantage linked to congressional action. This disadvantage might argue that while Congress is currently in bipartisan agreement on a critical issue, the Affirmative plan would destroy those alliances.

Solvency net benefits argue that the counterplan will solve the harms of the 1AC in a more efficient, cost-effective, or otherwise superior way. This is a single-pronged attack where the Negative team can win the round with the counterplan, but any argument made against the Affirmative's solvency will also hurt the counterplan. There are two reasons to use a solvency net benefit rather than a disadvantage net benefit. First, less time is needed to present one piece of solvency evidence for the counterplan than an entire disadvantage, which has at least three pieces of evidence. Second, solvency net benefits are easy for the Negative to win if they have an excellent piece of evidence that compares two ways to solve 1AC harms and concludes that the counterplan is superior in its action recommendations.

Types of Counterplans

The most basic types of counterplans are agent counterplans and advantage counterplans. These counterplans are so designated by the alterations they propose for the text of the Affirmative plan: the agent counterplan changes the agent of action; the advantage counterplan finds a different way to solve the advantage scenario(s).

AGENT COUNTERPLANS

Negative teams can choose one of five agents to enact a counterplan: Congress, the president (via Executive Order), the Supreme Court (via overturning a previous decision), state action, or a foreign government or organization. The only universal limitation to agent counterplans is that the plan and counterplan cannot have the same agent of action. In rounds with an agent counterplan, the judge determines a winner based on her assessment of which agent, plan or counterplan, will have the greatest implementation success.

Agent counterplans are common when debating resolutions that designate the U.S. federal government as the Affirmative actor. These resolutions allow the Negative to argue that another part of the U.S. government, a foreign government, or nongovernmental organization should implement the plan. Consider the 2011–2012 resolution:

> Resolved: The United States Federal Government should substantially increase its democracy assistance for one or more of the following: Bahrain, Egypt, Libya, Syria, Tunisia, Yemen.

This resolution mandates that the Affirmative act through the U.S. federal government. The Affirmative might present the plan: "The

United States Federal Government should substantially increase its support for civil law training programs in Yemen." The Negative team could offer a counterplan with another agent. For example, "The Republic of India should substantially increase its support for civil law training programs in Yemen." The net benefit for this counterplan could be a disadvantage arguing that any U.S. involvement in the internal affairs of Yemen will raise tensions and risk regional conflicts. Or, the net benefit could argue that the Yemeni people prefer Indian training programs. At the end of the round, the judge will address two important questions. First, can the plan and counterplan be implemented concurrently or are they mutually exclusive? Considering our example, can't the United States and India simultaneously provide civil law training? If the judge finds that the plan and counterplan are mutually exclusive (cannot happen at the same time), then she asks which, the plan or the counterplan, has the greatest benefits and fewest harms? The answer will determine the winner of the round.

STATES COUNTERPLANS

A special form of the agent counterplan is the states counterplan. This argument proposes that each of the 50 states enact the Affirmative plan simultaneously in lieu of national government action. State counterplans are usually supported by a disadvantage net benefit of federalism. The federalism disadvantage argues that having the national government enact the plan will upset the balance of power between the national government and the states. Enacting the plan through the states will restore the balance of power and prevent further consolidation of power at the national level.

A debate about a states counterplan focuses on two solvency questions: Can the states enact the plan better than the federal government? Will the states be willing to do so? When arguing a states counterplan, Negative teams cross-apply all of the 1AC's evidence and then provide one or two cards indicating that the states are equally or more qualified to implement the Affirmative's plan. The Affirmative will often concede that some states might be better equipped and more qualified to enact the plan than others. However, they will focus on the second question: Do states have the political will to act? The Affirmative will argue that while some states will enact the plan, other states will only enact the plan if they are mandated to do so by the national government. At the end of this debate, the Negative will have argued that endorsing action by the 50 states is more beneficial overall than the plan because it will have prevented consolidation of power at the national level. The Affirmative will have argued that the plan must be uniformly enacted and enforced across the nation, which only the federal government can ensure. The judge will evaluate both the solvency and net benefit arguments and name as winner the team with the greatest chance of solving with the fewest negative side effects—determined by disadvantages and advantages.

Advantage Counterplans

Advantage counterplans do not attempt to address the entire 1AC. Instead, they provide an alternative means of achieving the most significant advantage of the Affirmative plan. Negative teams use this type of counterplan when they are prepared to debate most, but not all, of the Affirmative advantages. The advantage counterplan proves that multiple avenues are available for solving a specific part of the 1AC. When successfully used, the Negative team argues that while the advantage is important, the 1AC is not the only or best way to solve the scenario. To win the round, the Affirmative must prove that it still solves for the other advantages in the Affirmative case.

Advantage counterplans are very popular when the overarching goal of the resolution can be met in various ways. Consider the resolution "Resolved: The United States Federal Government should establish an energy policy requiring a substantial reduction in the total nongovernmental consumption of fossil fuels in the United States." This resolution has several overarching goals, including increasing renewable energy production and decreased dependence on foreign energy markets.

A possible plan text under this resolution might read: "The United States Federal Government should increase funding for solar energy production." The Affirmative case contains three advantages: decreasing oil purchases from Saudi Arabia, stabilizing the energy grid, and decreasing greenhouse gas emissions.

The Negative team is prepared to debate the energy grid and greenhouse gas advantages. However, they have not researched purchases of oil from Saudi Arabia. When they review the 1AC evidence during preparation time, they learn that the Affirmative authors advocate decreasing oil purchases from Saudi Arabia as much as possible with the goal of ending purchases altogether. The Negative realizes that they could use this evidence to support an advantage counterplan that states: "The United States Federal Government should cease purchasing oil from Saudi Arabia." To present this counterplan, the 1NC cross-applies all of the Affirmative's advantage evidence to prove that decreasing oil purchases from Saudi Arabia is a good idea. Then, the 1NC introduces a generic disadvantage claiming that any new government expenditures (such as the Affirmative's recommending increased funding for solar energy production) will lead to a recession. This disadvantage serves as the net benefit to the counterplan because the Affirmative plan for federal funding of solar panels risks a recession while the counterplan does not.

Additionally, this net benefit shows how the plan and counterplan are mutually exclusive. Without the disadvantage, there is no reason why the federal government could not both increase funding for solar panels and cease purchasing oil from Saudi Arabia. With the disadvantage, however, the federal government cannot enact both the plan and the counterplan because doing so would lead to recession.

Status of the Counterplan

Negative teams have three options in advocating the counterplan: they can argue it "unconditionally," "conditionally," or "dispositionally." These options assume that the 2NR should advocate a single worldview (status quo or counterplan) to reject the Affirmative. The following table defines these terms and explains their function.

The Negative presents the counterplan:	What it means:	The Negative should choose this strategy when:
Unconditionally	The Negative will defend the counterplan throughout the debate, regardless of the Affirmative's arguments. If the Affirmative proves that the counterplan is less desirable than the plan, the Negative loses.	The Negative intends to defend the counterplan as the best policy option in the 2NR.

Conditionally	The Negative can stop advocating the counterplan at any time regardless of the Affirmative's arguments and default to defending the status quo.	The Negative intends to advocate either the status quo or the counterplan in the 2NR. They will make this decision after the 1AR.
Dispositionally	Under certain conditions, which the team will determine during the debate, the Negative reserves the right to abandon the counterplan.	The Negative lacks confidence in the counterplan or net benefit. Or the plan was vague and the counterplan can be used to force the Affirmative to clarify the differences between the plan and counterplan, thus possibly making them admit to linking to an argument such as a disadvantage or Kritik.

Answering a Counterplan

The Affirmative team has two goals when answering a counterplan—defend the ability of the plan to solve the harms and prove that the counterplan will not solve all of the Affirmative's harms. The Affirmative achieves the first goal by answering the Negative's solvency arguments. To accomplish the second goal, the Affirmative uses a combination of three strategies:

1. **Attack the net benefit**, eliminating any reason(s) why the counterplan solves more scenarios than the plan.

2. **Attack the "status" of the counterplan.** The status of the counterplan addresses how the Negative team presents the counterplan. Before offering a counterplan, the Negative has the burden of defending the status quo. After presenting their counterplan, the Negative must determine if they will defend only their alternative policy or both the status quo and the counterplan. To attack the Negative's advocacy, the Affirmative first determines what the advocacy is and then presents theoretical arguments against that choice.

3. **Make a "permutation" to the counterplan.** Permutations are theoretical arguments asserting that the counterplan and the plan are not mutually exclusive and that both can be adopted simultaneously.

To better understand how the Affirmative utilizes each of these strategies, consider the 1AC plan text:

> The United States Federal Government should increase funding to secondary education science courses.

The 1NC reads an agent counterplan:

> The 50 states should dramatically increase funding for scientific innovation.

The 1NC net benefit to the counterplan is that state action allows for a broader spectrum of funding, thus promoting more varied research.

ATTACKING THE NET BENEFIT

Affirmative teams attack the net benefit(s) of a counterplan by proving that the Affirmative case harms are greater, more important, or more likely to occur than the net benefit scenario.

Remember, to win the debate, the Negative team must prove that the counterplan is superior to the Affirmative plan. If both the plan and counterplan are good ideas, the Affirmative will win. Accordingly, the Affirmative need only prove that the net benefit is slightly smaller, less important, or less likely to occur than the Affirmative case. In the example of funding scientific innovation, the Affirmative could argue against the net benefit by proving that federal action is the only way to produce tangible results. State action might allow for more varied research but not meaningful innovation.

CHALLENGE THE COUNTERPLAN'S STATUS

The Affirmative can argue that Negative's counterplan is unfair because it allows them to defend either the counterplan or the status quo at the end of the debate. This type of argument is called a "moving target." These claims hold the most merit if the counterplan is presented conditionally or dispositionally. Challenging the status of the counterplan begins during cross-examination when the 2AC asks the 1NC to explain the status of their counterplan. The Negative's answer is considered binding—if the 1NC says the counterplan is conditional, the 2NC cannot change this status later in the debate.

The 2AC should challenge any counterplan that is presented conditionally or dispositionally. This argument will claim that the counterplan is abusive to the Affirmative because she could spend half of the 2AC arguing against the counterplan and the 2NC could drop the counterplan without any explanation. Like many theory arguments, challenging the counterplan's status seldom wins the round unless the Negative team does something exceptionally egregious such as claiming they are defending the counterplan unconditionally and then dropping the counterplan to defend the status quo in the 2NR. Arguments against the status of the counterplan do, however, have merit as a tiebreaker in a close round where the judge would have liked to have more Affirmative analysis of a particular argument. By challenging the counterplan's status, the Affirmative is able to explain any problems with their argument time allocations during the round.

PERMUTATIONS

Permutations are tests of competiveness in which the Affirmative attempts to prove that the plan and counterplan are not mutually exclusive (and could be implemented concurrently). Just like the Affirmative plan text and the Negative counterplan text, the permutation must be made in a written form that the judge can read at the end of the round. The two common forms of permutation are "do both" and "severance." By using these standard arguments, teams are able to create a permutation using only a few seconds of preparation time.

"Do Both" Permutation

Do both permutations advocate all of the plan and all of the counterplan. Using our secondary school example, the 2AC could present the following do both permutation:

> The United States Federal Government should increase funding to secondary education science courses and dramatically increase funding of scientific innovation.

This permutation forces the Negative team to defend the necessity of increasing funding for scientific innovation and explain why increasing funding for both secondary education and scientific innovation is impossible.

Severance Permutations

Severance permutations advocate part of the Affirmative plan plus all or part of the counterplan. For example, the 1AC reads a plan text:

> The United States Federal Government should fund humanitarian efforts in Columbia, Peru, and Chile.

The 1NC reads a counterplan text:

> The United States Federal Government should fund humanitarian efforts in Columbia and Peru.

The 2AC reads a severance permutation:

> The United States Federal Government should fund humanitarian efforts in Columbia and Peru.

The severance permutation text and the counterplan text are identical. Both remove funding to Chile from the 1AC Plan text. This permutation prompts a theoretical argument that will determine who wins this round. The Negative argues that part of the Affirmative plan (funding Columbia and Peru) is a good idea but that funding Chile is bad. The Affirmative's permutation argues that the judge could still vote for the Affirmative plan and just not fund Chile. Winning this type of permutation is difficult because most judges believe that the Affirmative must defend the entire plan throughout the debate.

You will hear a great number of counterplans throughout your debate career, some generic and some very specific. Counterplans force debaters to think about all of the intricacies of their plan and the many alternatives that might achieve the same goals. By focusing on the nuances of the plan and counterplan texts, you will become a stronger debater for both the Affirmative and Negative. Such close scrutiny will help you to spot round-winning differences between advantages and net benefits and quickly craft permutations.

KEY CONCEPTS

1. Counterplans allow the Negative to argue that other policies would solve the status quo's harms better than the Affirmative's plan.

2. To win a counterplan debate, the Negative must prove that the counterplan is preferable to both the Affirmative and the status quo.

3. To be competitive, counterplans and the Affirmative plan must be mutually exclusive.

4. Most counterplan texts will include some or all of the Affirmative plan text.

5. Agent counterplans propose the same policy as the Affirmative but endorse action from a different agent.

6. Advantage counterplans provide an alternative means of solving some or all of the Affirmative advantages.

7. The Affirmative can respond to a counterplan by disproving the net benefit, objecting to the status of the counterplan, and by offering a permutation showing that the counterplan and the plan are not mutually exclusive.

16

KRITIKS

Critical arguments, commonly called "Kritiks," are philosophical criticisms that focus on the Affirmative's language or assumptions rather than on the effectiveness of the Affirmative's plan and case. Debaters who focus on political issues argue that the federal government *should* or *should not* take an action to remedy a problem in the status quo by utilizing existing political structures. In contrast, Kritik debaters argue about what individual debaters *ought* to do, even if that includes taking no action or maintaining the status quo. The Kritik's focus on "ought" is grounded in the perspective that the words used in debate shape a debater's perception of the world. Therefore, changing the words and assumptions used in debate can have significant effect on how debaters approach both debate and the world beyond the debate round. Kritiks can be presented by the Affirmative or Negative team. Affirmative uses of the Kritik as a 1AC are discussed in

Chapter 10. This chapter will focus only on Negative Kritiks and methods used by Affirmative teams to answer Kritiks.

Kritiks are among the most complex arguments in policy debate, and some coaches argue that novice policy debaters should not use or even learn about them. These coaches contend that the philosophical preparation necessary to use a Kritik correctly is overwhelming for debaters who are just starting tournament competition. Other coaches, however, encourage novices to use Kritiks in their first round. They argue that Kritiks have become a fundamental part of policy debate and novice debaters should be able to choose the strategy that best fits their own interests and style. Even if you do not intend to present a Kritik, you will have to debate against opponents who do. Therefore, we recommend that all novice debaters understand this type of argument.

Kritik Basics

Kritiks are philosophically based arguments used by debaters to challenge their opponent's fundamental assumptions—that part of an argument that is presumed to be true but is never explicitly proved to be true. These assumptions are revealed by the words spoken by the debaters and the ideologies that have crafted the debaters' arguments. The assumptions addressed by a Kritik are varied; they may focus on just one word or might address the Affirmative's implicit support for a social or economic system. All Kritiks are designed to challenge an opponents' way of thinking about the resolution and the debate round.

Kritiks were developed by debaters and coaches frustrated by the limitations of policy debate. They were looking for a way to investigate the resolution beyond asking if the Affirmative case was better than the status quo. This led first to radical counterplans, such as the anarchy counterplan, which endorsed the disbanding of the federal government. These counterplans expanded the strategic options available to Negative teams, but were also very susceptible to permutations because they still embraced a policy-making approach. Kritiks became a separate argument when they began to address the philosophical assumptions within a debate. This refocused the debate round from a place to analyze specific policies to a deliberation about the act of debate and policy making.

Debaters use Kritik arguments for four reasons:

1. Kritiks shift the focus of the debate by arguing that radical alternatives, such as revolution, are preferable to pragmatically minded politics. As a result, Kritiks force the Affirmative team to explicitly defend political reform.

2. Kritiks are philosophical; they expose participants to new ideas and provide a forum to discuss rights, values, and responsibilities.

3. Kritiks promote critical thinking skills that are useful for socially active students and citizens.

4. Kritiks remind debaters and judges that the debate round influences the way real-world policy is created. Kritiks challenge the way that debaters use fiat and argue that this practice creates a preference for expediency rather than encouraging reflective decision making.

The variety of reasons for using a Kritik has produced three unique categories of Kritik: Kritiks of debate, rhetoric, and values.

Kritiks of *debate* challenge community assumptions about rules and standards by examining the role or potential role of marginalized arguments and voices in the debate round or community.

Kritiks of *rhetoric* challenge the use of language that is sexist, bigoted, or otherwise problematic in the debate round or in the debater's evidence.

Kritiks of *values* challenge the ethical contradictions or positions that have created the foundation of the opponent's arguments.

Regardless of the Kritik's goal or category, they should be presented as early in the round as possible, usually in the 1NC. While presenting a Kritik in the 2NC is permitted, many judges see this as a strategic trap designed to overburden the 1AR rather than an attempt to genuinely investigate a philosophical issue. Therefore, when Kritiks are presented in the 2NC, they should be introduced by explaining what action in the round has justified the new strategy. For example, if the 2AC made sexist remarks, then presenting a Kritik of his language in the Negative block is acceptable. Additionally, while you can present multiple Kritiks in the same round, judges usually prefer a solid, in-depth discussion of one Kritik rather than a superficial presentation of several.

Kritik warrants are found in philosophical texts, usually with a more verbose style of writing and a more complex vocabulary than that found in government reports or newspapers. Accordingly, Kritik cards are usually longer than those used to support a disadvantage or solvency argument. In addition, because of the argument's complexity, Kritiks are typically delivered at a slower pace. It is not unusual for a 1NC to present one Kritik that takes the entire nine-minute speech or to spend most of the 1NC presenting a Kritik alongside a few short topicality violations.

The Structure of the Kritik

Kritiks must contain a link and an implication. Some Negative teams also choose to include an alternative for their Kritik.

LINK

Kritik links identify a flaw in the Affirmative's case, philosophical position, or presentation. It is not uncommon for the Negative team to identify several links in the 1NC or to identify more links as the round progresses. All links must be supported by warrants from evidence or by analytical warrants that are supported by cross-applications from the Affirmative's evidence.

Philosophical Links

Philosophical links are derived from specific words in the case evidence or the philosophical position taken by the Affirmative's authors. For example, an Affirmative case with an economy advantage would link to a negative Kritik against capitalism because the Affirmative advantage presumes that a free-market economy is an advantageous socioeconomic system for all citizens.

Presentation Links

Debaters can also link a Kritik to their opponent's presentation style. For example, a presentation link is often used when an opponent speaks so fast that the other debaters cannot meaningfully compete in the round. While speaking quickly in a debate round is acceptable to many judges, debaters using this link claim that the speed of debate has become a tool of exclusion, making it hard for students to enter policy debate. This link is usually identified when only one or two of the debaters in the round can speak quickly and the others cannot understand or answer their opponents.

IMPLICATION

The Kritik implication argues that the Affirmative's flaw is significant and will become worse if the Affirmative team wins the round. Kritik debaters use evidentiary warrants to explain how the Affirmative makes the flaw worse or prevents society from correcting the flaw. Many implications are systemic, meaning that they are already present in the status quo, but could become worse. For example, racism, sexism, and classism are all common systemic implications. Other implications include poverty, oppression, slavery, dehumanization, and marginalization.

ALTERNATIVE

The Kritik alternative explains how a judge's ballot can be used as a symbolic endorsement of an alternative mode of thinking. The alternative begins by reminding the judge that Kritiks of the Affirmative's language and assumptions should be analyzed before debating the feasibility of the case. The Negative argues that even the best plan will not actually be enacted when the round ends. The discussion and criticism that occurred throughout the debate, however, will have real effects on future debates. Finally, the Negative explains that by voting for the Kritik, the judge will indicate her support for this process of critical investigation.

The three common types of Kritik alternatives are: rejection, rethinking, and using the ballot as a tool. These alternatives explain to the judge how to analyze the Kritik and clarify the differences between the Affirmative and Negative positions.

> *Rejection alternatives* argue that the judge cannot morally or ethically vote for a policy (such as the Affirmative plan) that promotes the form of discrimination identified in the flaw.

Rethinking alternatives ask the judge to vote Negative as a way to force the Affirmative team to rethink their assumptions or presentation. This alternative argues that without critical investigation of motives and actions, policymaking may do more harm than good.

Ballot as a tool alternatives argue that voting for a philosophical argument sends a message to the debate community that the rules of debate, which are often taken for granted, should be questioned. As a result, debate will become accessible to a broader array of students and audiences.

Framework: How Do Judges Compare a Kritik to an Affirmative Plan?

Frameworks are methods debaters propose for comparing claims, especially those that follow from different paradigms. Paradigms are the sets of values around which Affirmative and Negative teams develop the rationale for their strategies. In a debate where both sides advocate different policies, the judge can weigh the respective policies without considering paradigms. In the case of Kritik debates, however, comparison is critical. Because most Kritiks develop philosophical ideas that challenge the biases of policymaking and because Kritik debaters make arguments about both their opponent's paradigm and argument claims, the judge cannot ignore the difference in underlying values of the debater's arguments. To convince the judge to support their side, each team must present and defend a framework.

Debaters must carefully choose their framework before the debate round and maintain only one framework per round. Both the Affirmative and the Negative teams must clearly outline the criteria the judge should use when she must choose between a policy proposal and a Kritik. The framework that you choose will determine what arguments the judge will analyze, the order of that analysis, and the compatibility of your arguments.

Debaters may choose between three frameworks: comparative policy, critical theory, and pure negation. Many debaters present a framework during the debate but do not indicate the framework's name. Therefore, you must pay careful attention to determine which framework they are presenting and what arguments are most likely to provide a winning response.

Comparative policy framework argues that the Kritik alternative functions similarly to a counterplan: the team that avoids causing the most harms and that claims the most advantages wins the round. Usually, the Affirmative proposes this framework to minimize the effects of the Kritik. However, Kritik teams who are debating against Affirmatives with small-impact scenarios sometimes propose this framework because it is the simplest for the judge to evaluate. Additionally, Kritik teams can benefit from this framework if they can present the alternative as a solution to the Affirmative's harms while simultaneously offering a better paradigm. For example, the Affirmative plan sends food aid to a small country. The Negative presents a Kritik arguing that food aid is a way for global hegemons to force poorer countries into a relationship of dependency with richer countries. As an alternative, the Negative argues in support for a libertarian policy that eliminates food aid, which ultimately allows smaller countries to integrate into the global market at their own pace. Like a counterplan debate, the Negative will win this round if they can defend the stance that libertarianism has enough long-term benefits to outweigh the harm done by the liberal paradigm of food aid.

Critical theory framework argues that the judge should not treat the Affirmative team's case as a statement that results in a policy. Under this framework, an Affirmative plan becomes an ideological declaration that must be discussed. Negative teams use this framework to argue that the Affirmative should not simply assume that the U.S. federal government can and should pass the plan. Instead, the Affirmative must justify why it is roleplaying as the federal government and why policymaking is necessary to solve the issues presented in the case. Under this framework, the Negative argues that the Affirmative team should investigate the assumptions underlying its reflexive use of the federal government. Debaters use the critical theory framework to approach debate as a micro-political act, arguing that politics is not only remote, formal activity that happens in Washington, D.C., but rather a civic process that includes student debate. A judge who has been persuaded to use a critical theory framework will evaluate the round based on arguments about educational benefits and the advantages of political advocacy in debate before analyzing any actions argued by fiat.

Pure negation theory claims that the Negative wins the round if they can prove at least one reason why the Affirmative is undesirable—be that a Kritik or policy argument. In contrast to the critical theory framework, pure negation theory does not require the Negative Kritik to be consistent with the rest of the Negative strategy. For example, a Negative team using pure negation theory could present both a Kritik of capitalism (arguing that working within a capitalist system will result in dehumanization) and an economy disadvantage (arguing that the Affirmative plan will destroy the economy and lead to war). Because the Negative has presented two contradictory arguments, the 2NR must clearly explain to the judge the order in which these arguments should be evaluated. The 2NR should also argue that presenting contradictory arguments was necessary to answer the Affirmative's plan. By using the pure negation theory, the Negative team has forced the Affirmative to defend both the merits of using a capitalist paradigm and that its policy will not destabilize the economy. The Negative will ask the judge to evaluate the Kritik first and, if it does not win the Kritik argument, to evaluate the disadvantage second.

Performative Contradictions

Using multiple frameworks usually results in a "performative contradiction," meaning that one of your arguments contradicts and links to another argument that you presented earlier. Debaters argue that performative contradictions are abusive because the Negative team calls for the rejection of a certain action or ideology while themselves performing that action or using that ideology. It would be abusive or a rigged game against the Affirmative if they lose the round for an action or ideology that the Negative team also advocates. For example, a Negative team reads a Kritik that argues for an Affirmative loss because their plan focuses on economics rather than the general welfare of humanity. In the same speech, the Negative offers a disadvantage saying that the plan is a bad idea because it will hurt the economy. These two arguments constitute a performative contradiction since the disadvantage uses the same assumptions that the Kritik claims should result in a loss for the Affirmative.

Performative contradictions do not only apply to contradictions between arguments, they can also apply to contradictions between how a team is acting and how they say others should act. If, for example, a Kritik alternative calls for everyone to become vegan, it can only be taken credibly if all the members of the Negative team are vegans. Thus, the Negative might lose on a performative contradiction if they are advocating veganism but wearing leather shoes at the debate.

Using a Kritik in a Debate Round

To learn how the different components of a Kritik work together, let's examine how a Kritik of debate, a Kritik of rhetoric, and a Kritik of value might be used by the Negative team.

USING A KRITIK OF DEBATE

Kritiks of debate challenge the Affirmative's fidelity to the rules and standards of the debate community. These Kritiks force the Affirmative to justify their adherence to community standards—for instance, switch-side debating or only debating issues pertaining to the resolution. For example, an Affirmative advocates a topical plan calling for an increase in funding conflict resolution in the Middle East. The 1NC then presents a Kritik of debate arguing that the resolution diverts attention from important domestic social issues, such as racism, in favor of mediating global conflicts. The link is the Affirmative's topical plan. The implication argues that forcing the Negative to debate the plan makes debaters complicit with a system of ranking that prioritizes international conflicts over domestic problems. Finally, the 1NC presents an alternative, arguing that the debate should focus on domestic problems, such as racism, rather than on the resolution. The 2AC can respond to this Kritik either by agreeing to the Negative demands and engaging in a new debate or by defending both the case and framework of the 1AC. The judge will evaluate the round by first determining who won the framework debate and then analyzing the arguments made using that framework.

USING A RHETORIC KRITIK

Rhetoric Kritiks respond to the actions and speech of the participants in a debate round. A common rhetoric Kritik is linked to the gender pronouns used by the opponent, such as an Affirmative case that uses the masculine pronoun "he" to describe all policymakers, debaters, or debate authors. The specific link for this Kritik could be found in a 1AC speech that refers to the Negative team (of female debaters) as "you guys." The 1NC can use an analytical link, referencing the 1AC's speech and then present an implication supported by evidentiary warrants to argue that gendered language re-entrenches institutional barriers that make it harder for women to participate in activities such as debate. This implication could be supported by a rejection alternative that argues that the judge cannot ethically vote for a team that excludes women from debate. Or the Negative team could use a ballot as a tool alternative to argue that by rejecting the Affirmative team, the judge will send a signal to the debate community that gendered language will not be tolerated in a debate round.

USING A VALUE KRITIK

Value Kritiks are used to argue against the ethical assumptions made by the Affirmative's evidence. One common example is the Kritik of technology. This Kritik links to the Affirmative's assumption that new forms of technology will solve a problem that has been created by technological dependence. For example, the Affirmative case claims that building more nuclear missiles will deter other nations from challenging the military authority of the United States. The Negative team presents the Kritik of technology in the 1NC using two links—an implication and alternative. The first link is analytical; the 1NC references the 1AC's evidence that assumes more missiles are necessary. Then, the 1NC presents an evidentiary link to argue that international tensions are caused by policymakers' reliance on technology rather than diplomacy. Finally, the implication argues that the 1AC's acceptance of technological dependence and desire to build more nuclear missiles give a false sense of control while ignoring serious environmental and humanitarian risks.

The 1NC might also present a rethinking alternative that rejects the Affirmative case in order to allow deeper consideration of our society's overdependence on technology. However, the judge's ballot is unlikely to affect the real-world development of nuclear technology and the manufacture of nuclear weapons. Therefore, a stronger Negative framework would be alternative advocacy. Using this framework, the 1NC could present a philosophical alternative to the plan, for instance, calling for programs that would strengthen diplomatic ties between nations. Because stronger diplomatic ties would remove the reason for needing more nuclear weapons, the Affirmative case and Negative Kritik alternative would be mutually exclusive. The judge would evaluate this round by comparing the Affirmative case and Negative Kritik alternative.

Affirmative Answers to the Kritik

Kritik answers begin in cross-examination when debaters use clarification questions to analyze the claims and evidence used to support the link, implication, and alternative. Then, the remaining cross-examination should be used to understand the Negative's framework. The information collected in cross-examination will guide the type and quantity of answers the 2AC must present. Three standard Affirmative strategies are available: defend the comparative policy framework, make permutations, or present a counter-Kritik. These strategies can be successfully used independently or in combination with one another.

DEFENDING THE COMPARATIVE POLICY FRAMEWORK

Policy and hybrid 1ACs use the comparative policy framework to argue that their plan is better than the status quo, any counterplan, or Kritik alternative proposed by the Negative. This is a useful tool for the 2AC because the framework clearly defines what arguments are and are not allowed in a policy debate round. To defend the comparative policy framework, the 2AC first argues that while the Kritik may be an important idea, a policy debate round is too short to produce a detailed analysis of the philosophical concept. This is also called a "wrong forum" argument because it suggests that other discussion formats, such as a college seminar, are better places to discuss Kritiks. Additionally, by maintaining the comparative policy framework, the 2AC is able to extend the Affirmative's harms and argue that the Affirmative team is equally concerned with the questions raised by the Kritik.

For example, let's assume that the Affirmative case contains an advantage showing that the plan fights human trafficking and the sex trade. This advantage includes a piece of evidence arguing that human trafficking and the sex trade are dehumanizing crimes commonly found in the status quo. The Negative team has presented a rhetoric Kritik linked to the Affirmative's misuse of gendered pronouns during the 1AC. The 2AC is able to argue that their case has been specifically designed to decrease human trafficking, thus leading to a more equitable and balanced society—the same goal as the Negative Kritik. The team that can most strongly defend their framework will be the winner of this round. If the judge accepts the Affirmative's comparative policy framework, the Affirmative will win the round because they prevent millions of people from being trafficked into slavery. If the Negative wins the framework debate, the judge will evaluate the necessity of preventing two people from using a gendered pronoun in a debate round and the potential that this Affirmative's loss will encourage future debaters to carefully consider their pronoun use.

MAKING PERMUTATIONS

Kritik permutations argue that it is possible to both vote for the Affirmative case and advocate the Kritik. The Affirmative uses this argument to prove that the Kritik is not mutually exclusive or is not a reason to reject the Affirmative. All Affirmative teams, regardless of their 1AC style (policy, Kritik, hybrid, or performance), can benefit from this argument for two reasons. First, permutations allow the Affirmative to defend two separate reasons for voting for the Affirmative; thus, the judge can now vote Affirmative either exclusively based on the merits of the case or on the merits of the case blended with the Kritik. Second, permutations make it easier to manage a framework debate. By arguing that the Affirmative case and Kritik can be combined, the Affirmative team can continue to use the comparative policy framework while gaining the benefits of the arguments proposed by the Negative team.

For example, the Affirmative presents the plan: the United States Federal Government should build more nuclear missiles aimed at securing American military hegemony. The 1NC presents a Kritik of technology linked to the Affirmative's presumption that more missiles (more technology) will resolve international tensions that were created by the building of earlier missiles. This Kritik alternative is to build diplomatic ties. The 2AC responds to the Kritik with a do both permutation, which argues that the plan and Kritik are not mutually exclusive. By using this argument, the 2AC can argue that in the short term more missiles must be built. However, greater attention should also be given to establishing and strengthening diplomatic ties, and, once those ties are strong enough, the U.S. federal government will no longer need nuclear missiles. This permutation proves that it is possible to both build missiles and diplomatic ties; therefore, the Kritik is not mutually exclusive and not a unique reason to reject the Affirmative.

PRESENTING A COUNTER-KRITIK

Counter-Kritiks allow the Affirmative team to agree that philosophical investigation is necessary while simultaneously arguing that the Negative's investigation is flawed. Hybrid and Kritik Affirmative teams are able to use this strategy without entering a framework debate because they have already moved away from the comparative policy framework. Policy Affirmative teams, however, must first concede the Negative framework and then present their counter-Kritik.

Counter-Kritiks are presented in the 2AC and have a strategic advantage of putting pressure on the Negative block to both defend their own Kritik and attack a new, complex argument from the Affirmative. To use this strategy, the 2AC presents a link, implication, and alternative for her counter-Kritik. In counter-Kritik rounds, the judge determines a winner by deciding which philosophical statement or position has been best debated according to the framework.

Affirmative teams are often prepared to present a counter-Kritik and include a piece of evidence necessary to develop it in the 1AC. For example, a hybrid Affirmative team debating the 2010–2011 debate topic calling for an increase in visas presents a case including an advantage that the plan solves human trafficking and the sex trade. Most of the evidence in this advantage discusses statistics and first-hand accounts by victims of human trafficking, but the advantage also contains a piece of evidence claiming that when policymakers refuse to debate about the sex trade they dehumanize people who have been trafficked and, in doing so, devalue all human life. This evidence is presented along with the other cards in the advantage. Before the round, the 2AC prepared to emphasize the argument's importance if the Negative team had presented a Kritik.

The 1NC then presents a rhetoric Kritik arguing that the Affirmative case contains male-gendered pronouns for female authors of the 1AC evidence. The Negative team argues that using gendered language is bad because it creates barriers to secondary education. The 1NC makes many other arguments, but does not discuss the 1AC's human trafficking advantage.

The 2AC responds to the Negative's rhetoric Kritik by extending the dehumanization evidence from the 1AC. This evidence is now a link for the Affirmative's counter-Kritik. The 2AC explains that the Negative, just like policymakers, has refused to debate about the sex trade. The 2AC then presents an implication, the Negative team has devalued the lives of people who have been trafficked and entered the sex trade. In this round, the judge will evaluate the implications of the gendered-language Kritik against the counter-Kritik of dehumanization. To win the round, the Affirmative does not have to prove that gendered language is an unimportant issue for debate, only that refusing to debate about the sex trade is worse than employing a gendered pronoun.

Conclusion

Kritiks are challenging but, with practice, they are also exciting. Outside of the classroom, you rarely find a forum in which philosophical arguments and radical politics are evaluated as alternatives to pragmatic policymaking. Whether you choose to present critical arguments or not, you will definitely have to respond to them. Instead of feeling overwhelmed, approach Kritik arguments as learning experiences. Many Kritiks are based on changing the way that we think about and analyze our world. The debaters presenting these arguments are often concerned both with winning the round and educating the judge and debaters about the Kritik. You can prepare for Kritik rounds by reviewing Kritik files and watching Kritik rounds. This will help you understand both the arguments and frameworks used in these rounds. However, don't overlook the opportunity to talk to Kritik debaters and coaches about their arguments, both during the round and outside of the tournament.

KEY CONCEPTS

1. Kritiks are philosophically based arguments that allow debaters to question the fundamental assumptions of their opponent's and provide reasons to reject the opposing team.

2. Kritiks have three critical parts: link, implication, and alternative.

3. Kritik links are formed from the Affirmative's case, philosophical position, or presentation.

4. Kritik arguments are judged by the framework in which they are presented. Both the Affirmative and Negative should present a framework and argue that their framework is superior by using the standards of fairness and education.

5. Affirmative teams that present a policy 1AC use the comparative policy framework.

6. Negative teams use one of three main frameworks to justify the Kritik: pure negation theory, post-modern or critical theory, and alternative advocacy.

7. Negatives should be careful not to make a "performative contradiction" or use arguments that link to their own Kritik.

8. Affirmatives may argue that Kritiks are inappropriate for policy debate rounds by making "wrong forum" arguments.

9. Affirmatives may compare the Affirmative plan and the Kritik alternative by making permutations and/or presenting a counter-Kritik.

17

JUDGING THE DEBATE

Policy debate is judged by a highly specialized pool of evaluators: professors and graduate students at the forefront of policy debate developments. Debating in front of these individuals can be thrilling, but it can also be very intimidating. To help you tame your nerves and win some rounds, this chapter will give you an overview of judging philosophies, preferences, etiquette, and how judges evaluate arguments. Obviously, we cannot predict how a judge will decide a round, but we can help you understand what a judge is expecting.

Judging Philosophies

Even though policy debate judges will consider a variety of different arguments, each judge has specific preferences for arguments and debate styles. Some judges form an opinion about an argument and stand by that opinion for several years, while other judges' opinions evolve with each round or after an enlightening round that caused them to view the subject in a new way. Rather than have to explain those changes at the beginning of each round or worse—keep debaters in the dark about their opinions—policy debate judges create judging philosophies (concise statements about how they judge a debate). Judging philosophies are available online for debaters to review before and during a tournament. This allows debaters and coaches to formulate their arguments for a specific judge and preferentially rank judges who will be at the tournament.

Most judges post their judging philosophies to the community board: http://judgephilosophies.wikispaces.com/. This site alphabetically lists most of the judges on the national circuit with their most up-to-date philosophy statements. This online tool is exceptionally valuable, but, as with all Internet resources, is subject to Internet access and availability. Don't assume that you will always have access to these philosophies at the tournament. Instead, prepare by printing out the philosophies of all judges who will attend the tournament or download them to the team computer for easy access before the round. In the rare event that you encounter a judge who has not posted her philosophy, don't be afraid to ask about her judging preferences before the round.

You need to know two pieces of information about a judging philosophy: what arguments does the judge prefer and what framework does the judge use. For example, some judges will write, "I have no specific preference; just make sure you explain the relevance of the argument you are making. I will use a policymaking framework unless you argue otherwise." In front of this judge, debaters can feel free to present any argument they choose. This judge is amenable to teams presenting disadvantages or counterplans. Negative teams who will present Kritiks are warned that they need to clearly articulate an alternative to the policymaking framework.

When a judging philosophy is short or vague, like the one above, make sure to ask your judge additional questions. While you are free to ask about argument preferences, be sure to phrase your questions to produce specific answers. For example, the question, "What do you think of conditional counterplans?" will produce much more useful information than a broad questions such as, "What's your judging philosophy?"

Knowing judging preference can be invaluable. If you know your judge's philosophy, you can tailor your arguments to ensure the best chance of winning the round.

Judge Preferences

After your first tournament, you will have a very good idea about what type of judge you like and what kind of judge you would prefer never to see again. Wouldn't it be great if you could use this information to control your judge assignments? You're in luck! Debaters submit preference sheets before all tournaments to help determine who will judge in each round. Ask your coach how your team submits these forms. Some squads submit one form for all of their teams; others allow individual debate teams to submit their own forms.

Preference sheets serve two functions. First, they determine who is not permitted to judge you. This includes both previous and current coaches and teammates. Second, they indicate who you don't want to judge your debates. You can use "strikes" against judges who are incompatible with your team's style of argumentation. For example, if you are a Kritik-oriented team, you will probably try to strike every judge who states, "I only vote on policy-based plan texts." Most tournaments set a limit on the number of strikes you can use. After you have used all your strikes, you will rank the remaining judges in order of preference.

Etiquette

The high threshold of debate experience required to become a policy debate judge produces a small pool of potential judges. Thus, your judges will be well-qualified and you will debate in front of the same judge many times. Because you will meet so frequently, establishing and maintaining an amicable relationship is critical. The following five suggestions have both helped us maintain good ties with our judges and are actions that we have appreciated when judging rounds.

1. Treat your judge as you would a professor or teaching assistant who is grading an essay. Respect that they have experience in the topic area, have a positive interest in your intellectual development, and are attempting to make a fair evaluation.

2. Maintain a judging notebook. After each round, ask your judge if she has any suggestions about how you could improve your debating style or your arguments. Write down all of this advice. Then, if you will be debating before her again, you can quickly review her advice and improve your performance.

3. Do not fight with the judge. Even if he is wrong, keep your cool until you are at least 500 yards away from the tournament, and then vent only to your coach, not to everyone in the immediate vicinity. If you react immediately after the round, the judge may hear you and some judges *will* take your comments personally. You will see this judge again, and you gain no benefit by being remembered as the annoying novice.

4. Don't be afraid to follow up on offers of help. Remember that a judge usually is also a coach and is well-trained to help you improve your debating skills. Follow through on his advice about what evidence to read, new authors to investigate, or speaking skills that need a tune-up. Of course, don't buck the advice of your coach and partner, but also don't be afraid to try something new.

5. Follow up on your own promises! If you say that you'll e-mail the judge citations, do it ASAP. Failing to fulfill promises will make judges remember you as the lazy debater who they shouldn't go out of their way to help.

In the Round

WHAT DOES THE JUDGE WANT?

Judges want debaters to make arguments that enable them to clearly explain who won and lost the debate. Consequently, they pay particular attention to rebuttal overviews, areas in the debate where Affirmative and Negative teams compare their arguments and explain why their team has won the debate. Judges do not want teams to merely read a lot of evidence. In fact, they become annoyed when debaters read additional evidence during a rebuttal instead of making comparative claims. Overall, judges will appreciate and vote for debaters who analyze arguments and evaluate evidence.

ADAPTING TO YOUR JUDGE

After reading your judge's philosophy, adapt to the judge. Style adaptations can be simple. If a judge indicates that she dislikes high-speed debate, then you know that you have to speak at a conversational pace to win the round. Argument adaptations are more difficult. Judges will often indicate what types of arguments they prefer. You don't have to present arguments that you are unfamiliar with just to please the judge. Instead, select a variety of arguments that reflect both the judge's preferences and your expertise. Presenting an argument well is better than presenting an argument poorly just to please the judge.

PRESENTING YOURSELF POSITIVELY

Judges are heavily influenced by the level of decorum in the round. Insulting the other team, being crude, excessive swearing, and yelling are all excellent ways to make the judge dislike you. Maintaining a courteous disposition is particularly important during cross-examination, when inexperienced debaters often find themselves yelling at each other. If this happens, stop. Remember to stay calm and polite. The judge will appreciate your self-control.

JUDGE'S NON-VERBAL LANGUAGE

Some judges will try to help you during your speech with non-verbal cues. For example, judges frequently make circular motions with their pen over their flow, indicating that they have heard enough of the argument you are making and would like you to move on. Judges also commonly nod in appreciation for well-presented arguments. These non-verbal cues are useful only if you look up from your speech, so don't keep your head buried in your arguments. Also, pay attention to the judge's body language during your opponent's speech. This can provide valuable indications of how your judge will evaluate the round.

The Reason for Decision

At the end of your round, the judge will fill out a ballot and submit it to the tabulation room to record her decision. This ballot has two parts. At the top, each speaker is assigned a number of points on a 1–30 or 1–100 scale and then ranked against the other speakers in the round. In the body of the ballot, the judge records the winner and a "Reason for Decision." Occasionally, a judge will write a long essay evaluating the round. More commonly, the judge will write a brief sentence, such as "voted Affirmative on the dropped turn on politics," and then give a lengthy verbal review of the round and her decision.

You must remain in the room while the judge completes the ballot. This can take some time, and the judge may ask to see various pieces of evidence presented during the round. Be prepared to give these to her quickly. If you desperately need to use the restroom, make sure that your partner is in the room. If the judge needs evidence and neither of you is there, she will either give up or angrily come looking for you. Neither is desirable.

Listening to the Decision

Listening to the decision is one of the most educational and difficult parts of a round. It is educational because a well-qualified individual is analyzing your arguments and giving you feedback about the strengths and weaknesses of your work. It is difficult because you have been deeply engaged in the debate and either you want to keep arguing your point or you want to get out of the room and far away from the arguments. Regardless, you must sit and listen to what the judge has to say.

Once the judge has reached her decision, she will either immediately announce who has won the debate or give a brief summary of the debate and the voting issues and then announce who won. Write down everything the judge says. Even if you just lost, you need to keep writing; the information about why you lost is just as important as if you had won. If you won, you also need to keep writing as your judge will identify arguments that need improvement.

Often debaters are eager to leave the classroom. Maybe lunch is about to begin, or it was the last debate of the day, or the next round is supposed to start in just a few moments. Regardless of the reason for your rush, resist the temptation to move about while your judge is speaking. This includes not packing your evidence or putting away your supplies until the judge has finished delivering her decision. She has spent one-and-a-half hours listening to you; now is the time to listen to her.

Following the decision, the judge will ask if you have any questions. This time is invaluable and will help you better understand the round and how the judge evaluated the arguments each team presented. If you do not understand an argument that your opponent made, feel free to ask the judge to clarify it for you. If you understood all of the arguments, then you can aim your questions at getting to know your judge and her decision-making criteria. Even if you do not have specific questions about arguments, ask for ways to improve your speaking style. If you are upset at the end of the round, you might want to ask if you could speak with your judge at a later time. Remember, judges were debaters, too, and know that losing can be hard. Finally, resist the temptation to fight with your judge. Most tournaments prohibit judges from changing their decision once the ballot is signed, so even if you could convince your judge that she made the wrong decision, she would not be able to change her ballot.

Low Point Wins

Sometimes the better-ranked speakers can lose the debate, resulting in a "low point win." This is rare and some tournaments do not permit it. Low point wins usually occur when the losing team was exceptionally persuasive as speakers but lost a major argument. The low point win allows the judge to record speaker points that accurately reflect the speaking skills of the debaters while still indicating who won the round. Because rankings are calculated first by the win–loss ratio and second by total speaker points, these decisions have an important effect on a team's overall ranking at the tournament.

Judging Panels

Elimination rounds are judged by panels of three or five individuals who best meet the preferences of both teams. Although the judges sit as a panel, they decide the round independently and sign individual ballots to record the winner. Then, they meet in the hallway to discuss how they evaluated the round and count the number of votes for each team. These judges are not permitted to change their decision based on the decisions of the other judges on the panel.

Unanimous decisions are announced by one of the judges, who will give a brief overview of the round, explain the panel's reasons for its decision, and then invite the debaters to speak privately with each of the judges. If the debate created a split panel, one of the judges will announce the decision (such as 1–2, 1–4, or 2–3) and identify which judges voted for which team. The judges voting with the majority will give a summary of their decision, and then each of the dissenting judge(s) will give his or her reasons for the decision. Both teams are then invited to discuss the decision with any of the judges.

KEY CONCEPTS

1. Review your judge's philosophy before the debate begins.
2. Treat your judge as you might a TA or professor, with respect and politeness.
3. Regardless whether you have won or lost the round, maintain good etiquette through the judge's decision by writing down the reasons for his decision and not fighting with the judge.
4. Pay attention to your judge's non-verbal signals during the round.
5. Quietly wait for your judge to complete her ballot at the end of the round and listen attentively while the judge explains her decision.
6. Listen closely to your judge's Reason for Decision, which will provide in-depth analysis on the arguments and speeches from the round.
7. Low point wins occur when the individuals who win the debate are given lower speaker points than their opponents.
8. Elimination rounds are judged by three or more judges, with the majority of votes determining the winner of the debate.
9. Follow up on any offers of assistance or requests from your judge ASAP.

18

YOUR FIRST TOURNAMENT

Debate tournaments are weekend-long events that require hours of preparation and travel. This chapter will help you anticipate the schedule for your first tournament and understand the preparations necessary to make it an enjoyable experience. Before the tournament, your main concern is dealing with school responsibilities and determining travel plans and communicating them to concerned individuals (usually your parents). During the tournament, you need to consider the daily schedule and your expected activities between rounds. Following the tournament, you should be concerned with both reviewing the tournament and making sure that you have caught up with your school obligations.

Before the Tournament

As with all forms of travel, preparation is paramount. Debaters will sometimes become so focused on their arguments and research that they forget the bare necessities required to attend a tournament. Knowing what is necessary when traveling will make your debate experience far more enjoyable and balancing your school and debate responsibilities easier.

SCHOOL ARRANGEMENTS

You MUST inform the professors of your Friday and Monday classes that you will be attending a debate tournament. Even if you expect to return to your university on Sunday night, you may be delayed, and it is much easier to make arrangements for absences before they occur. Remember that you are academically obligated to make up all assignments and exams you miss if your professor permits. Some professors do not allow make-up exams, so check before you commit to a tournament. Before leaving for the tournament, you should organize your weekend assignments into work you can do while traveling (reading and flashcards) and work done best at a desk (researching and paper writing).

TRAVEL ARRANGEMENTS

All debate squads make their tournament arrangements collectively, and many squads pay for all of their members' travel expenses. Debaters usually travel to tournaments in vans driven by their coaches, stay in hotels with same-sex members of their squad, and eat meals either at the university in which the tournament is held or in restaurants near the campus. Usually, you will not have to register yourself for the tournament or find a hotel. If you have specific dietary or housing needs, prior to embarking you need to be proactive in ensuring that arrangements are in place.

Your parents appreciate knowing your travel plans. If the coach hasn't provided specific information about lodging and the tournament schedule, ask her for it. Informing your parents of your plans will prevent them from franticly searching for you over the weekend. Notify your roommates and significant others as well. Debate tournaments are all-day events, and you will not be able to use your cell phone and Facebook account consistently. By giving advance warning of your absence and inability to communicate, you can prevent a lot of frustration and worry.

Partner Coordination

Before departing for the tournament, you and your partner need to agree on who will bring the debate materials and supplies. Making a checklist of what you need—files, pens, flow paper, etc.—will both save time when you are packing and ensure that you always arrive at the tournament ready to debate.

You and your partner might want to discuss what you will wear during debate rounds. Coordinating your wardrobe is an important part of making a good impression during the round. The debate community does not require a specific style of dress, although some squads do, so check with a coach. Some debaters wear suits, while others wear jeans and T-shirts. Whatever your style, you must coordinate with your partner. You will look poorly organized if one debater wears a suit and the other wears jeans.

At the Tournament

Although debate tournaments are held at a different university each weekend, they adhere to the same schedule. So that you are prepared for the weekend, we will review both the day-by-day schedule and the schedule of a single round.

On Friday, teams meet early in the morning and drive to the host university. They aim to arrive in the early afternoon with enough time to change their clothes at the hotel before reporting to the tournament for registration and the first two debate rounds. Dinner is often served at the university between the first and second rounds. Debaters return to their hotel after the second round to prepare for their next day of debate, complete schoolwork, socialize, and sleep.

Saturday morning begins with an early breakfast at the hotel. Four rounds of debate follow, beginning around 8:30 a.m. and finishing in the late evening. Lunch is served at the university between the fourth and fifth rounds of the tournament. Dinner is after the sixth round, either at the university or at a restaurant near campus. An awards ceremony may be held in the evening. If not, announcements about which teams will go to elimination rounds will be made at the tournament hotel and online.

Sunday morning begins with early breakfast at the hotel and transportation to the tournament. Teams competing in elimination rounds report to their assigned rooms. The other debaters either watch elimination rounds, work on research arguments (both for teammates in elimination rounds and in preparation for future tournaments), or study. Even if no one from your squad is debating in elimination rounds, your coaches are obligated to judge Sunday's first round. Squads depart once they have been eliminated and all judging obligations have been fulfilled. Because each team will leave at a different time, awards are distributed at the end of each elimination round. Teams end the day by traveling back to their university, usually arriving in the late evening.

Because all tournament participants stay in the same hotel, eat in the same places, and sometimes travel together, you must be careful when discussing your team's debate strategy. Many squads adhere to the 500-yard rule, meaning that if you are within 500 yards of another debate team, you should not discuss your debate strategy in a voice above a whisper. You should also not discuss your opinions of your opponents, your judge, or any other tournament-related subject. These conversations are best held in vans and closed rooms.

Debate Round Schedule

Before each debate round, the tournament organizers will distribute a schematic of debate assignments. The schematic will indicate whether you are Affirmative or Negative, the names and schools of your opponents, your judge, and the room assigned for debate. Schematics are typically distributed 30 minutes to an hour before the round begins. This gives you time to meet with a coach, discuss your strategy, and move your debate materials to the assigned classroom.

Once both teams have arrived, the Affirmative will disclose their plan and advantages, and both teams will continue working with their coaches until the round begins. Once the judge arrives, you will have time to ask about his judging preferences. Do not expect judges to arrive early, however; they are also coaches and will be preparing with their own teams. Note that time is not built into the schedule for Affirmative disclosure or pre-round discussions with coaches or judges. The amount of time for these activities is determined by the the number of minutes between when everyone is in the room and when the schematic indicates the 1AC should begin speaking.

The debate round proceeds without interruption—no bathroom or cell phone breaks. If you need to use the bathroom or step outside to get some water, make sure to ask the judge before leaving. After the 2AR, you will shake hands with your opponents and begin organizing your materials. The judge will evaluate her flows and may request evidence from either or both teams. Do not leave the room until the judge has delivered her decision. Even if rounds are running late and the next round should have started before your judge reaches her decision, do not leave the room. Tournaments have student assistants assigned to either keep judges on schedule or to reorganize the schedule. Your job is to stay in the room and pay attention to the judge's decision.

When the round is over, wait for the next round's schematic or follow the tournament's instructions about meals or returning to your hotel.

After the Tournament

Congratulations on making it through your first tournament! We hope you enjoyed it. Now, call your parents, catch up with your school assignments, and work on improving your debate skills. Once your family and school obligations have been met, make an appointment with an assistant coach or older debater. At this meeting, you should review your experience, revise your argument strategies, and discuss any partner issues that arose at the tournament. Even experienced debaters follow this post-tournament routine; it keeps them from becoming overwhelmed by schoolwork and ensures that they are prepared for their next tournament.

KEY CONCEPTS

1. Your family obligations and schoolwork always come first. Make sure that you understand and have met these obligations before participating in a debate tournament.

2. Squads collectively organize travel arrangements and tournament registration.

3. Debate tournaments are all-day, Friday through Sunday, events.

4. Debate opponents, judges, and rooms are assigned for each round and announced by a schematic or a chart distributed by the tournament organizers.

5. Adhere to the 500-yard rule during the entire tournament and do not discuss your team's strategy within the hearing of your competitors.

6. After returning from a tournament, first follow up on all family and school obligations and then meet with a debate coach to prepare for your next tournament.

19

"OH SHIT" LIST

As a novice, you may sometimes find yourself in an unanticipated situation. To help you get through such moments, we have compiled advice on a list of scenarios that might make you exclaim "Oh shit!" while frantically trying to resolve a problem. In the following pages, you will find recommendations on topics ranging from partner issues, conflicts during a debate round, judge and coaching problems, and a collection of miscellaneous issues that might arise during your debate career. No one will experience all of these problems, but everyone has lived through a few of them. Regardless of the situation you find yourself in, don't panic!

Partner Issues

My Partner Did Not Show Up

Sometimes, because of an illness or an emergency, your partner may not attend the tournament. If this happens, first inform your coaching staff; they might already know about the absence, but it's best to make sure. Now take a deep breath . . . you have three options that allow you to still attend the tournament.

First, most tournaments will have some of their debaters on standby for just this situation. You then can debate as a "hybrid team."

Second, you could debate by yourself, which is known as "going maverick." This is an exhausting way to debate, and tournaments only allow it in extreme circumstances. Additionally, most tournaments place limitations on maverick debaters, such as permitting them to win debate rounds but not advance to elimination rounds.

Third, you could scout for your squad. In this case, you would not debate but rather attend rounds between teams that your team wants to know more about. Maybe you know that University X has a new Affirmative. You would watch their round, take copious notes, and report back to your squad both about University X's new case and how the Negative responded.

Whatever option you choose, remember that this is a temporary problem, so make sure to keep it in perspective.

I HATE My Partner

Yeah, he really is a jerk, isn't he? Take a deep breath. Sometimes you have to debate with someone you don't like for a tournament or two. Over time you might decide that he's not so bad or that his skills are so good that you can deal with his personality. If not, talk to your coach. She might switch your partner or suggest a meeting among the three of you to discuss any issues.

My Partner Hates Me

First, figure out why she hates you. Are you working too hard? Not enough? Many debaters—particularly novices—can become too competitive during rounds, and this can be misinterpreted as anger or hostility between partners. Try to determine the problem and talk it over with your partner after the round or the tournament. Keep in mind that being confrontational or acting without thinking first will only make things worse.

In the Round

The Other Team Has Eight Tubs Full of Evidence and I Only Have Thirty Pages—I Have No Hope of Winning!

Not true! Don't be daunted if another team seems to have a lot more evidence than you do—often it's an intimidation technique. Chances are that they don't know most of their files very well and aren't prepared to present any more arguments than you are. They might even be carrying around empty tubs! Stay positive and keep in mind that while you don't have as many files, you are completely familiar with your arguments.

The Room Has Only One Table and the Other Team Is Sitting at It

You have a few options. First, is the judge in the room? If so, ask the other team to share. Most likely they will not want to appear overly aggressive in front of the judge and will make space for you.

If it's just you and the other team, still ask how they plan on sorting out the space and request at least half the table to speak from. This is not unreasonable. You do need a place to speak, and it has to be a stable surface. If that doesn't work, sit on the floor. Camp out with a wall of tubs in front of you, spare tubs for mini-desks, and as much prep space as you need. When the judge asks why you are sitting on the floor, just answer honestly: your opponent refuses to share.

We Forgot to Read Our Plan Text in the 1AC

Read it in the 2AC. The 1NC might emphasize that you don't have a plan and therefore should automatically lose the round. But think back, did you disclose the plan before the round? If so, then they have seen the plan and your mistake did not destroy their strategy. Even if you did not disclose your plan text, did you honestly answer questions from the 1NC? If so, then you are still in good shape. Your only concern is preventing the appearance that you strategically omitted the plan text to throw off the Negative's strategy.

Begin your 2AC with a statement such as: "In this speech, we will present our plan text. We disclosed this plan before the round and none of the words in the plan text have changed between then and now. We do not believe that our failure to read the text in the 1AC was abusive because the Negative has already seen the text. Failing to read the text was a mistake, not an attempt to disrupt the round." Mistakes happen, and this one is not large enough to destroy your chances of winning the round.

Time Ran Out in the 1AC Before We Got to Solvency

DON'T PANIC! They call the 2AC a constructive speech for a reason. When the 2N asks you why you have not discussed solvency, just let them know you will be doing so in the 2AC. Don't beat up your partner or apologize profusely. The Negative team may argue that by not reading solvency you have destroyed their strategy. However, you did present arguments in the 1AC. The Negative should be able to develop quality arguments from that evidence, and they can still read their solvency arguments in the 1NC.

I've Never Heard of the Argument That the Other Team Is Presenting

This is a problem for all debaters, not just novices. Occasionally a new argument will pop up and confuse you. Make sure that you get all of the other team's cards as they are read so that you can start analyzing the argument. Even if you do not have evidence to refute their claims, you can always make analytical arguments. Don't be afraid to spend most of your time during CX asking basic questions such as how their argument links to yours, what are the impacts to their argument, and how the judge should evaluate the argument. It may seem strange to ask your opponents to help you understand their argument. However, think of it from your opponents' point of view—these clarifications are an excellent way to show off their knowledge of a specific argument. These are questions that they can answer easily, and they will probably receive high speaker points for answering them politely. On the other hand, if your opponents refuse to answer these basic questions, that will clue both you and the judge into the fact that they do not understand their own arguments.

I Am Not Prepared for the Other Team's Argument

You have two options. First, you can carefully examine their evidence. Are there logical fallacies in their claims? Do all of their authors agree? How old is the evidence and is it still accurate given today's political climate? You probably know your own arguments well, so start creating claims and analytical warrants addressing why your opponent's evidence simply does not apply to your specific scenario.

Second, you can present parallel arguments. These arguments do not answer your opponent's claims, but they do match impact for impact. For example, an Affirmative team who has no answers for a disadvantage that leads to mass extinction should poke holes in the Negative's evidence and read a new advantage that claims to prevent extinction. At the end of the round, the Affirmative will have presented the judge with a compelling case, including an advantage that prevents extinction. The Negative will have claimed that the Affirmative case causes extinction, but to win their claim they will have to offer analytical arguments against the disadvantage and the Affirmative's new advantage.

I Have No Idea What the Other Team Is Talking About

It happens! Use cross-examination to figure out what's going on. Don't be shy. Even if you spend all of your time just figuring out what they said, it's time well spent!

I Just Realized My Partner and I Are Presenting Different Strategies

You should have agreed on strategy before the round, but confusions can happen to the best teams. Confusions like this almost never occur on the Affirmative, so this advice is directed only to Negative teams. What you should do when you realize that your arguments contradict is determined by whether you realize the problem before or after the 1NR.

> **If it's before the 1NR:** Take some prep time to determine how this confusion occurred. Did the 2NC read from the wrong file, are you just misunderstanding the round, or have the two

of you become confused about what your strategy should be? Don't waste time pointing fingers. Rather, determine what your strongest argument is. The 1NR should now argue for that and stop supporting any arguments that would contradict that argument.

If it's after the 1NR: First, have you made any unconditional arguments such as counterplans or Kritiks? If so, you must continue debating these positions. The job of the 2NR is now to win the counterplan or Kritik and to explain why the contradictory arguments were merely tests of the Affirmative, not the Negative's true arguments.

If you haven't made any conditional arguments, the 2NR should decide which arguments he can best explain. He should prepare a compelling story about how those arguments function in the round and are superior to the Affirmative's. His partner can help with these preparations by determining what offensive arguments, permutations, and theory arguments the Affirmative has made and ensuring that the 2NR is prepared to quickly address and dismiss those arguments.

Whatever you do, DO NOT have a loud conversation about this strategy problem. A smart opponent will pay close attention to your fight. They might even carefully take notes on your arguments and gain an advantage by knowing what you will present in the 2NR.

They Made Me Promise to Go Slow, and Then Talked Really Fast!

First, think about what's happening. Was there a misunderstanding about what "fast" means? Is the other team very nervous and speaking fast but also mumbling? Is one of your opponents very fast but his partner is struggling to get even a few words out?

Has significant damage been done or can you recover and pick up your own pace?

Chances are the judge has paid attention to the varying speeds in the round and will award speaker points accordingly. Slower teams can beat faster ones, so if you think the round can go on, tough it out and win by making smarter arguments.

If you suspect that the other team intentionally deceived you, you can persuasively argue that they violated an ethical standard of debate. This argument is made in an overview in the next speech. When giving the roadmap, indicate whether the judge needs to use a new piece of paper or a new Excel spreadsheet to flow the overview. Then, once the speech begins, you will present a two-part argument. First, the violation: your team radically changed styles to accommodate the other team, and your opponents took advantage of your courtesy. Second, the voter: ask the judge to stop the round and immediately vote for you. Realize that the voter is an overstated claim. Unless something is seriously wrong, the judge will not stop the round, but she will take the violation into consideration at the end of the round when determining a winner. This violation may not result in your winning the round, but it could serve as a critical tiebreaker to determine a close round.

My Solvency Author Is a Hack for X Organization

Okay, sometimes your evidence doesn't come from the most qualified or respected sources. Remember that policy debate draws from a variety of scholars, government officials, think tanks, and mass media. Each of these has a particular bias. If your evidence makes sound claims backed by logical warrants, it is not terrible. If your opponent argues that the judge should ignore your evidence because it is from a biased source, address this issue but also take time to emphasize the quality of your evidence.

The Other Team Stole Our Evidence!

Are you sure? Have you checked every possible place, including the trash can, your backpack, and your pockets? If so, how did the "theft" occur? If you were in a rush to pack up for your next round and they ended up with your file by mistake, then just find them and ask for it.

If you saw them take your evidence, pack it up, and they then denied having it, you will need a bit of help to get it back. Talk to your coach and explain the situation. Your coach can then talk to the other team's coach. If you need the evidence back immediately for your next round and your coach is nowhere in sight, then ask your opponent's coach for assistance. Don't accuse your opponent of theft. Simply say "Hi, we debated your team in the last round and we are pretty sure that they packed up our 1AC by mistake. Can you help us get it back?"

This advice assumes that the other team took a paper copy of something during the round. Debating paperless requires that you let your opponent see everything that you read during the round, often by transferring files to a viewing laptop via a flash drive. Even though your opponent could copy all of the evidence on the drive, the debate community has elected to work on the honor system and train debaters to access only the files indicated by their opponents. Do not waste time worrying about what your opponents are doing with your evidence, but do pay attention to how much access your opponents have to your evidence. You should only share the evidence that is pertinent to the debate round and not the entire file of research. You can make sure that you do not share too much by putting the arguments you will use in a new electronic document and including only that document on the flash drive or viewing laptop.

Also remember that a good team will record the author and source of everything you read. It is very likely that every team at the tournament has a copy of the killer card you read yesterday. This is not theft, just good research skills.

I Left My Tubs at the Tournament

Tell your coach ASAP. Even if you are already in the van and even if you are already in a different state. Your coach might be able to find a team that is still at the tournament and ask them to pick the tubs up for you. Or you might have to turn around and retrieve them. Either way, you'll need to give out some pretty big thanks once you get them back.

I Am Crying!

Excuse yourself, find a bathroom, and take the time you need before reappearing in public. Debating is a high-stress activity. You are not the first one to cry, and anyone who makes fun of you is an idiot.

Judge Issues

The Judge Doesn't Have a Philosophy

Sometimes judges will forget to put their philosophy on the judging philosophy index before the tournament begins. This is more common with newer judges who are still trying to establish how they judge debates. Don't be afraid to ask! Most judges are happy to clarify their thoughts about various debate arguments before the round starts. Also feel free to ask questions before the debate if you know the judge has a philosophy but you are unable to get online to look at it.

I Think the Judge Is Asleep

You can use two approaches to this problem. If the judge is actually asleep, talk to the other team. Together you should appoint one person to go find some coffee or water. When that arrives, wake up the judge and kindly offer the beverage.

Hopefully, you will be able to catch sleepiness before it turns to sleep. If your judge walks into the round looking tired, offer to find some pre-round coffee. If he starts dozing off, play with your tone and pace during the speech. Try using the judge's name. You'll do a better job getting his attention if you say "and our judge (insert judge's last name) should vote . . . "

After the round say something quietly to your coach. You should not embarrass the judge (he will just dislike you), but it is helpful and safety-conscious to let someone know. A judge who was falling asleep in a round needs to rest before driving his team home. A lot of your judges are graduate students who will stay up all night researching for their debaters, drive all day to the tournament, and then start judging rounds. Overwork does not excuse sleeping during your debate, but understanding that it is the workload, not your speech, might make their sleepiness easier to handle.

I Know That Sound . . . My Judge Is on Instant Messenger During My Speech!

Unfortunate, but it happens. Some judges get distracted when they've already heard the arguments you're making. This is particularly common during the 1AC or 1NC because your judge may already have heard your arguments while judging another team from your squad and might even have a flow of your speech. Paying attention 100 percent of the time is hard if a judge has heard the exact same arguments round after round. Take this problem as a challenge to improve your delivery skills. Start emphasizing critical words and varying your speed and pitch to grab his attention. You can't do much during the round, but you should talk to your coach after the round and consider adding this judge to your strike list.

We Lost the Evidence That the Judge Is Calling For

This happens more than you would expect. First, make sure that the evidence is really lost by sorting through every file used during the round. If that doesn't work, check your files, flow paper, or any other paper in the immediate vicinity of your team's supplies. Check the trash. Finally, ask the other team to look for the paper. They might have accidentally picked it up during the round. Don't accuse anyone of stealing your evidence. This will make you look desperate, and the judge will be deterred from asking for other pieces of evidence that could have swayed her decision in your favor.

If, after checking the entire room, you still have not found your evidence, you can get a copy from another team in your squad. Finding lost evidence can take some time, so let your judge know that you are still looking for it. If you have to leave the room to find another team, send only one debater. The other team member should stay in the debate room in case the judge asks for any other pieces of evidence.

The Judge Acts Like He's Best Friends with the Other Team—I Feel Like I'm Going to Automatically Lose.

Don't be too worried. All judges are required to fill out a sheet of "constraints" against debaters who they have taught, coached, or debated with. If you are convinced that the judge has treated you unfairly, tell your coach after the round.

The Judge Is Dating a Member of the Other Team

Then he should have recused himself from the round. However, it's not always possible to do so. Don't despair! The judge is probably aware that voting for his significant other will look suspicious. This could give you a slight advantage in the round.

I Dated the Judge

If you parted on bad terms, you should have struck the judge. Alternatively, you can ask the judge (your ex) to recuse herself from judging your rounds. Either way, this strike is referred to as a "judging constraint" and does not count against your strike quota. If your relationship ended amicably, then your ex is allowed to judge you. You probably know a lot about the judge's argument preferences and have a good shot of winning the debate.

The Judge Is an Idiot

We would like to tell you that your perception of the judge is the result of miscommunication. Maybe he is extremely intelligent in a discipline with which you are unfamiliar. Or maybe she is an excellent critical thinker who has trouble expressing herself. Unfortunately, sometimes the judge really is an idiot. In the world of debate, you have to constantly adapt to new judges, so embrace that idiot. Discover what kind of arguments she likes and use them. You may think you are wasting your time, but you'll find idiots everywhere you go in life. Learn to deal with them.

Coach Issues

I Don't Have a Coach

It's okay! Debaters often find themselves without coaches. Whether you are on a squad without coaches, your coach couldn't make it to the room to help you before your round, or your university is in between coaches, don't worry. When you don't have a coach, paying close attention to your judge's advice is extremely important. Take notes, ask questions, and don't be afraid to follow up after the round or tournament has ended. The debate community is a very open, and people are always willing to help you even if they are from a different university.

My Coach Yelled at Me

If you suspect that your coach is about to yell at you, have the confrontation in a public place. Both you and your coach are members of a tight-knit community, and hopefully your coach will moderate his voice if he knows his peers are observing him.

Remember that some coaches are 22-year-old graduate students with little more experience, but a lot more responsibility, than you. If you just totally messed up, you might be in for a confrontation with a very stressed out person. If both you and your coach are overwhelmed by the situation, find an older coach, even if it's from another team, to help you sort out the problem.

Don't yell back and don't panic. If you are being yelled at, your coach is either overly invested in your competitive record or you did something inappropriate and immature. Take a deep breath and take his points into consideration.

Other

I Can't Afford a Laptop

You are not alone. The cost of laptops is one of the most pressing issues in the transition from paper-based to paperless debate.

If you are still debating with paper, don't worry about finding a laptop. Teams that debate paperless must have a laptop for their opponents to use throughout the round to access their evidence. They should also explain how to use the laptop and help you with any problems caused by the laptop's hardware or software.

You will need a laptop if you are debating for a paperless team. Arrange a private meeting with your head coach to discuss this problem. Admitting that you can't afford a laptop can be embarrassing, and you don't need to do it in front of the whole squad. Ask what she suggests you do. Could you work for the squad to earn enough money for a laptop, borrow one from the school, or debate paper-based until you can acquire a laptop? Also ask if your school is enrolled in any federal programs to help students afford computers. You might be surprised.

I Don't Want My Mom to Watch the Round

Technically speaking, you can't stop her. That being said . . . there are ways. First, determine *why* you don't want your mom to watch. If it's because her presence will make you super-stressed, tell her that her attendance will affect your ability to debate. If it's because you're afraid of being the weird kid with his parents watching, don't worry. It's increasingly common for parents to watch a round to better appreciate why their child (and their money) disappears every weekend. In most cases, they watch one round and realize they can't understand a thing. They leave quickly, yet fulfilled.

If you are vehemently against your parents watching, have this conversation well ahead of the tournament. Allowing your parents to travel to hear you speak and then not making them welcome in a round is simply mean.

I Feel Sick—I Think I Might Throw Up

Debate can be a nerve-wracking activity. Take some deep breaths and remember that while this is an academic activity, it is also a game. Over time you will become more comfortable.

I Heard a Rumor That . . .

It's really easy to get swept up in rumors. Do most of them matter? Not in the slightest. Avoid the rumor mill, but if you hear something that concerns or troubles you, consult your coach or an older debater.

I Really Need to Finish This Assignment

Hopefully you'll never have to miss a debate tournament because you have to complete schoolwork. However, you should be prepared to always put your schoolwork before your debate schedule. If you are afraid that going to the tournament will ruin your grade or prevent you from finishing your work, tell your coach ASAP. She needs to cancel your registration or find a replacement so that your partner can still attend the tournament. You or your coach might be able to negotiate an extended deadline for a paper, but this is a dangerous habit and these requests should be reserved for true emergencies.

In the future, take time to organize your schoolwork. Traveling to debate tournaments can take hours, and you can complete some tasks such as reading and flashcard/memorization in the van or on a plane. You can also bring your research materials to the tournament and work on an assignment during breaks between rounds or at night in your hotel. Remember that everyone on your squad is a student and will, or at least should, respect your need for a quiet space to complete assignments. Finally, find ways to study with your teammates such as drilling each other in preparation for an exam or proofreading one another's essays.

My High School Arch-Rival Is Now on My Squad

Ah, the nemesis. This situation is not uncommon. For better or for worse, you will now be spending a lot of time with this individual. After a few weeks of awkwardness, you may discover that you are both reasonable, fun people who can get along. This can take time, so don't panic if you are not best friends by the first tournament. If you have serious problems with each other, consult your coach on how best to handle the situation.

Debate Has Consumed My Social Life!

Debate can be time-consuming, but it does not have to prevent you from enjoying other activities. When you join a squad or enter a new partnership, you should be open about how much time you're willing to commit to debate. Coaches don't get angry when you discuss limits for your commitment. They do get annoyed if you stop attending meetings or tournaments with no prior warning. Your coach puts a lot of her free time and energies into work for the debate squad under the assumption that you're doing the same. When your priorities change, you should be open about your decisions and help your coaches avoid needless work.

Also, keep in mind that debate can *be* your social life. Most debaters subscribe to the idea of work hard, play hard—most novices are surprised to discover that a debate party is more than sitting around discussing dead philosophers (though that does happen sometimes). Give the debate social arena a shot;

if you don't like it, you'll have no regrets about moving on to something new.

I Want to Join a Fraternity/Sorority, Too!

Well, that's an interesting life choice and could create scheduling problems. The Greek life typically requires a significant commitment of time. Unfortunately, participation in policy debate requires just as much commitment. Talk to both and make sure that, when combined, your schedule is reasonable for both groups. Depending on how active your fraternity or sorority is, you might be able to continue participating in both activities. If not, you will have to choose. Remember that, above all else, you are a student first. Don't overcommit yourself and risk failing out of school.

I'm a Novice . . . and a Senior

Welcome! Your life as a debater should be no different from the freshman on the team. Even if you're only in debate for one year, you'll be amazed at how much you can develop as a debater in a short time. Don't stress about your graduation year—just enjoy yourself!

APPENDIXES

Appendix A: Speaking Drills

This appendix will help you improve your speaking style. While these exercises are designed help you in debate, their focus on enunciation and extemporaneous argument are also very helpful for your daily life. If you are new to debate, or haven't done drills for a long time, don't despair; we've identified the problem for which each drill is useful, so diagnose your speaking symptom and look below for the cure!

Note that you should perform each drill for 10 minutes even though the longest debate speech is 9 minutes. That way, you'll become accustomed to talking for longer than your speech time and won't be gasping for air during CX.

PEN DRILL

Good For: Separating words, clarity

Side Effects: Slobbery pen

Materials: 1 CLEAN pen, 10 minutes worth of text

Procedure: Place the pen sideways into your mouth, pushing back until it rests in the crevices of your lips and your tongue has to push against the body of the pen. Proceed to read the text out loud, making sure to fully enunciate each word. You'll find that you cannot read nearly as fast as usual and that your tongue has to do a lot of extra work to make the words intelligible. This is the point of the drill. Read continuously for 10 minutes, take a break, and repeat if desired.

Some debaters find that they overly salivate on the pen during this drill. If this happens, don't end the drill. Instead, quickly clean the pen and begin again. Thanks to your saliva, you have the opportunity to train not only for enunciation but also for enduring distractions during a speech.

ALPHABET

Good For: Stretching your mouth before a round, clarity
Side Effects: Funny faces
Materials: Just you!
Procedure: Say the alphabet as clearly as possible twice through. Say each letter to its fullest. Make your mouth as open as possible and stretch your neck into the letters until the tendons and muscles in your neck stand out and feel weird. You don't need to be loud, just keep a normal speaking voice. Your mouth should feel stretched by the end of the exercise.

This is a nice quick drill to get over the "I just woke up" feeling before the first round.

BACKWARDS

Good For: Clarity and speed
Side Effects: Sounds ridiculous
Materials: 10 minutes worth of text

Procedure: Start at the end of the text and read each word from the bottom of the right corner to the top of the left corner. Yes, you are reading the text backward and no one will be able to understand what you are saying. However, you also have to focus on each word and look directly at the text. You don't know what word will come next, so you cannot skim or read too fast.

This drill works well for debaters who are starting to get a little too sure of themselves and skipping words in an attempt to go faster. It is also good if you are experiencing a "dyslexia feeling" that the words are not coming out of your mouth in the proper order. By upsetting your normal reading habits, this drill enables you to refocus on clearly delivering the entire text.

EVERY LETTER

Good For: Slurring, mumbling
Side Effects: You might learn how to spell
Materials: 10 minutes of text
Procedure: Read each letter of the text. R-e-a-d-e-a-c-h-a-n-d-e-v-e-r-y-l-e-t-t-e-r-o-f-t-h-e-t-e-x-t. This drill can be frustrating, and you won't be able to go as fast as you would like. However, you will be able to prevent your judge from calling "clear!" in your next round.

A DRILL

Good For: Slurring, mumbling
Side Effects: Sounds like pig Latin

Materials: 10 minutes of text

Procedure: In this drill, you insert an "a" between each word. This drill is much less difficult than the "every letter" drill. While the "every letter" drill is more helpful for building endurance, it can be frustrating. The A drill, however, is easier and will boost your confidence for your next debate round.

THE PLEDGE

Good For: Controlling your breath while talking

Side Effects: You might turn blue

Materials: Kindergarten attendance

Can you say the Pledge of Allegiance without taking a breath? Good! Can you say it twice? How about three times? Four? Once you can get to three or four times, you will have reached the average for a policy debater's lung capacity. Please be careful; if you don't usually exercise, you may get lightheaded pretty quickly!

Appendix B: Cross-Examination Cheat Sheet Guide

The following is a list of typical questions in the order that you should ask them during cross-examination. You do not need to follow the list like a recipe; if you already know the answer to a particular question, you can skip it, but do not be afraid to work through the entire list. Also, look for ways to incorporate your own questions as they develop throughout the round.

2NC ASKS THE 1AC (POLICY)

1. May I see your plan text?
2. How do you define _____?
3. What are the qualifications of your solvency authors?
4. Your solvency authors wrote in ___(year)___; how do you explain the lack of attention their proposals received between then and now?
5. How much will the plan cost?
6. What is your plan's enforcement mechanism?

2NC ASKS 1AC (KRITIK)

1. May I see your plan text?
2. What is your reason for not presenting a plan text in this round?
3. What framework do you propose the judge use to evaluate this round?

4. What is the role of the Negative in that framework?

5. If all Affirmative teams used the framework that you suggest, would it still be possible to have policy debates, and, if so, how would those debates be different from the round that we are having now?

1AC ASKS 1NC (DISADVANTAGE)

1. What is the internal link for the disadvantage?

2. Would you explain the steps between our plan passing and your Impact occurring?

3. What is the framework for the disadvantage?

1AC ASKS 1NC (TOPICALITY)

1. What are the voter issues for the topicality violation?

2. Can you name 10 cases that would meet your violation?

3. What is the source of your definition for your topicality violation?

1AC ASKS 1NC (KRITIK)

1. What is the text of your alternative?

2. How will this round achieve the alternative?

3. What is the status of the Kritik?

4. Can you explain how you define the status of your Kritik?

5. What will the world look like once the alternative is achieved?

1AC ASKS 1NC (COUNTERPLAN)

1. May I see your counterplan text?
2. How are you running the counterplan (conditionally or dispositionally)?
3. How do you define (conditional/dispositional)?
4. What is the net benefit to the counterplan?
5. Where is the solvency for the counterplan?
6. What is the inherent barrier to the counterplan?
7. What parts of the 1AC will the counterplan solve?

Appendix C: List of Abbreviations

The following list of abbreviations results from the debate community's desire to use complex terminology in a rapid speech.

The most important use of abbreviations is between two debate partners. Because you and your partner need to understand each other's flows, you need to coordinate your abbreviation style. Debaters frequently fine-tune abbreviations to meet their individual needs, so beware of over-abbreviating during conversations with other debaters. You might come across as needlessly excluding those who have not yet learned the abbreviations or worse—as a person who is lacking linguistic skills.

Speakers
1AC—First Affirmative Constructive
1NC—First Negative Constructive
2AC—Second Affirmative Constructive
2NC—Second Negative Constructive
1NR—First Negative Rebuttal
1AR—First Affirmative Rebuttal
2NR—Second Negative Rebuttal
2AR—Second Affirmative Rebuttal

Other
Ø—No/Null
Ⓚ—Key (Critical)
!—Impact
!/T—Impact Turn
A2—Answer(s) to
Adv—Advantage
Aff—The Affirmative case read in the 1AC.
Alt—Alternative to the Kritik
Anthro—Anthropocentrism

Arg—Argument
ASPEC—Agent Specification
AT—Answer(s) to
Biz Con—Business Confidence Disadvantage
Condo—Conditionality
CP—Counterplan
CX—Cross-examination
DA—Disadvantage
Dedev—De-development (economic collapse)
Dispo—Dispositionality
Ebsco—Ebsco Host (Digital database)
Econ—Economy
Elim—Elimination Round (e.g., double-octos, octos, quarters, semis, finals)
Ev—Evidence
Expando—Accordion file for holding evidence
Ext—Extinction
H—Harms
I—Inherency
I/L—Internal Link
IL/T—Internal Link Turn
ISPEC—Implementation Specification
K—Kritik (Critique)
L/N—Lexus-Nexus (Digital Database)
L—Link
L/T—Link Turn
Muse—Project Muse (Digital Database)
Neg—The Negative case read in the 1NC
N/U—Non-unique
OSPEC—Over-specification
OV—Overview
OW—Outweigh
Pltx—Politics Disadvantage

PoMo—Postmodern
Prelim—Preliminary Round
Quals—Qualifications, especially those of a piece of evidence
Res/Rez—Resolution
Spec—Specify (v.) or specification (n.)
Spread—Speed Read
T—Topicality
T/—Turn
U *or* Uq—Uniqueness
USFG—United States Federal Government
WMD—Weapon(s) of Mass Destruction
X—Extinction
XO—Executive Order Plan or Counterplan mechanism

Appendix D: Paperless Debate

Increasingly, teams are "going paperless," meaning that they store all of their evidence on laptops. Supporters expect that the entire debate community eventually will adopt this system, which saves both paper and the space needed to carry files to tournaments. Even if you do not plan to debate paperless, you should know the basics so that you are prepared for paperless opponents. Remember that paperless debate is evolving. It is bound to change over time, and you will have to keep up with these changes. Like all aspects of debate, how evidence is shared and distributed is completely open for discussion—so don't be afraid to consider new possibilities!

NUMBER OF LAPTOPS

Although each squad and debater must determine their optimal paperless setup, the debate community has reached the consensus that paperless teams should have three laptops. Obviously, the two debaters on a paperless team will each need a laptop to look at their evidence, so that's two laptops. Why a third? The opposing team has the right to review all of the evidence presented in the round. Since debaters do not want to constantly pass laptops back and forth, paperless teams bring a third, "viewing laptop" to each round. Some teams also find bringing a small printer to a tournament useful in case their opponents or the judge have trouble reading off the computer screen.[1]

---

1. For an extended study of paperless debating in action, see Whitman University's Debate Template Guide, "How To Paperless Debate," available at: http://www.whitman.edu/rhetoric/tech/paperless-complete-manual.pdf

PRESENTING EVIDENCE

You must consider a number of issues when organizing your evidence digitally, including evidence size, context, formatting, and compatibility.

1. **Size Matters**—Simply because you can edit font size does not mean it's a good idea. Debaters want the font size of their evidence readable. As a rule, don't make your font any smaller than 8 point Times New Roman. Often, debaters will shrink the words that they aren't reading, but making them too small isn't fair. It destroys the context of the evidence and, while opponents could increase the font size, they would have to do so during their preparation time, distracting them from analyzing the evidence and creating arguments.

2. **Context, Context, Context**—Going paperless doesn't change the need to provide context for your evidence. Make sure to include at least the beginning and end of the relevant paragraphs you are using. Without this context, opponents and judges might be suspicious of the claims in your evidence since they don't know the intent of the original author.

3. **Too Much Information**—Too much context is too much of a good thing. If you are using three paragraphs from a book, you don't need to cut and paste all 300 pages of the original text into your file. Stop a card where it is appropriate and feel free to ask for help from your coaching staff or a fellow debater if you are uncertain about what to include. Debaters commonly help one another with these kinds of issues.

4. **Well, Isn't That Fancy?**—Formatting your evidence in "Gill Sans Ultra Bold Condensed" font might look great on your computer, but it likely will cause problems in the round. First, fonts must be easily legible. Second, your evidence files must

be quickly accessible on a variety of computers using both Microsoft Word and Open Office software. Digital debaters typically use commonly available fonts such as Times New Roman or Arial in case someone's computer does not have the necessary font. Once you have selected a font, you need to be consistent among files.

5. **Not All Computers Are Created Equal**—Not all computers may be able to do what yours can—so don't get too fancy. Just because your computer has software that can easily read, edit, and display a PDF document doesn't mean that your viewing laptop will have this. As a rule of thumb, keep all cards in .doc or .docx (Microsoft Word) format and refrain from including any pictures (screen captures, etc.) in your document.

6. **With Tech Breakthrough Comes Breakdown**—Make sure to carry an "old-school" paper copy of your 1AC, several copies of your plan text, and few generic 1NC arguments for policy and critical Affirmatives. Even though each team has three laptops, you need Plan B. Make sure these copies are with you at the tournament—not in your hotel room.

ORGANIZING A PAPERLESS SYSTEM

Paperless debaters use Word documents and system folders to organize their evidence. Most debate squads store a "master" set of evidence on a private server. Debaters then copy these Word files onto their own computers and then edit them. Many of the norms and practices for paperless debate are still being established, but the best form of organization to date is as follows:

1. Create a Word document for each file using short and direct file names such as "Varsity 1AC" and "Economy Disadvantage."

2. Once you have enough files that it becomes difficult to navigate through them, you should create sub-folders (or sub-directories). Each folder should contain a specific type of file, such as "Affirmative case," "Counterplans," and "Disadvantages."

3. Place all of these sub-folders (sub-directories) in a master folder (directory) known as the "Virtual Tub." This directory should contain all the files you might need while debating.

Appendix E: Resources

Below is a listing of other policy debate resources that we think are interesting and innovative. Remember, every aspect of policy debate is open to interpretation. Look at some other interpretations, talk to your coaches and teammates, and don't be afraid to try new things!

BOOKS

Edwards, Richard, *Competitive Debate: The Official Guide* (New York: Alpha, 2008).
   A comprehensive handbook on Lincoln-Douglas, policy, and public forum debating styles for both high school and college debaters.

Ericson, Jon M., and Bud Zeuschner, *The Debater's Guide*, 4th ed. (Carbondale: Southern Illinois University Press, 2011).
   This book explains the theories underlying debate, both in relation to collegiate policy debate and everyday construction of claims and warrants.

Louden, Allan D., *Navigating Opportunity: Policy Debate in the 21st Century* (New York: International Debate Education Association, 2010).
   A chronicle of the proceedings of the 3rd National Development Debate Conference. This book provides detailed analyses of the state of intercollegiate policy debate in America.

Snider, Alfred, *Code of the Debater: Introduction to Policy Debating* (New York: International Debate Education Association, 2008).
   A guide to high school policy debate, including strategies and arguments also used in collegiate debate.

WEB-BASED GUIDES AND MANUALS

Brushke, John, "The Debate Bible." No date. http://commfaculty.fullerton.edu/jbruschke/debate_bible.htm

>Outlines what debaters need to prepare against varsity college policy teams. Divided into 10 books, Bruschke addresses the six keys to preparedness: tech, cards, and theory about disadvantages, the Kritik, topicality, and counterplans.

Prager, John R., "Introduction to Policy Debate." Last modified 2002. http://webpages.charter.net/johnprager/IPD/IPDindex.htm

>Prager breaks the college policy debate round speech-by-speech. Especially helpful for debaters who want to conceive a purpose for each speech they deliver.

Wake Forest University, "Debaters Research Guide." Last modified 2007. http://groups.wfu.edu/debate/MiscSites/DRGArticles/DRGArtiarticlesIndex.htm

>A comprehensive resource with links to theory articles written by leading debate coaches from 1979 to 2007. Especially helpful for debaters who want to historically ground their understanding of debate rules and norms.

WEBSITES FOR POLICY DEBATERS

CEDA Debate
http://www.Cedadebate.org

>The Cross Examination Debate Association (college level). Website hosts a forum to discuss debate topics, tournaments, and future resolutions.

Cross-X.com
http://www.cross-x.com
> Aimed at the high school debate community. Provides discussion boards for a variety of debate topics. Also sells evidence.

Open Case List
http://opencaselist.paperlessdebate.com
> Open access wiki with the most up-to-date information about every university debate team that regularly attends tournaments.

Planet Debate
http://www.planetdebate.com
> Designed for the high school debate community; provides some public access educational resources including video lectures on a variety of arguments. Sells evidence.

Tabroom.com
https://www.tabroom.com
> Information about tournament registration, judges, and tournament results. Both college and high school listings.

GLOSSARY

Advantage—the part of the 1AC that explains the benefits of carrying out the plan.

Advantage counterplan—a counterplan that proposes a different way to solve one of the Affirmative plan's advantages.

Affirmative (Aff)—the team assigned to propose an action that supports the resolution.

Agent—the institution used to enact the Affirmative plan or Negative counterplan. The agent is often a branch of the U.S. federal government.

Agent counterplan—a counterplan that has the same action as the plan but uses a different agent.

Agent specification (A-spec)—a theoretical argument that accuses the Affirmative of not adequately identifying the agent that will enact the plan.

Analytical argument (Analytic)—a warrant presented using only the debater's own reasoning and explanation (as opposed to a warrant from evidence).

A priori—a term used to indicate a specific argument in the debate round that should be evaluated before all other arguments.

Ballot—the judge's written record that indicates the winning team and speaker points for each debater in a given round.

Brink—an evidence-based argument that magnifies the implication of an advantage or disadvantage. This argument claims that the advantage or disadvantage scenario is on the verge of happening and that a small action will cause the scenario to occur.

Card—a quotation from an academic publication, periodical, or government document. This quotation is used as evidence during the debate round.

Case—the series of arguments for the resolution offered in the 1AC, status quo.

Cite—a citation of a card. The citation includes the author, publication, press, and page numbers or web address.

Clash—a point of conflict between Affirmative and Negative arguments.

Conditional—a theory argument used by the Negative team to justify the abandonment of a counterplan or Kritik.

Constructive speech—the first four speeches of a round; used to outline the initial arguments of the Affirmative and Negative in a debate.

Counterplan (CP)—a Negative argument that presents an alternative to the Affirmative plan. When using a counterplan, the Negative team accepts that the status quo is flawed, but argues that an action different from the Affirmative case will solve best.

Cross-apply—a shorthand means of referencing an argument made elsewhere in the debate without having to repeat the warrant or re-read evidence.

Cross-examination (cross-ex, CX)—a three-minute question-and-answer period that takes place after each constructive speech.

Disadvantage (disad, DA)—a Negative argument that claims the Affirmative's plan will create political or economic problems.

Dispositional (dispo)—a theory argument used by the Negative to justify the abandonment of a counterplan or Kritik if certain conditions are met. These conditions are determined by the debaters during the debate.

Double-turn—a strategic mistake made when a team turns both the link and the impact of a scenario resulting in creating support for the opponent's argument.

Even if—a logical calculation used in rebuttal overviews. It explains why a team should win "even if" the opposing team wins some or all of their arguments.

Evidence—quotations from journals, newspapers, books, reports, and government documents that are used as the warrant for a claim.

Expando—an accordion file folder that is used to organize debate files.

Extension—an elaboration or reiteration of a previously presented argument.

Fiat—the assumption that the Affirmative plan will be adopted. Using fiat allows debaters to debate the desirability of the plan, rather than the likelihood that the plan will be approved by the agent. Fiat is Latin for "Let it be done."

File—an indexed collection of arguments organized into shells, frontlines, and extensions that help debaters to defend their side of an argument.

Flow—a technical form of note-taking that allows debaters to keep track of the complex arguments presented by both teams in a debate round.

Framework—a set of standards used by debaters to explain to the judge how arguments in the debate should be evaluated.

Frontline—a set of analytical and evidentiary warrants prepared before the round and used to refute a specific argument.

Ground—the division of arguments about the resolution between the Affirmative or Negative teams.

Harms—the part of the 1AC outlining the harmful conditions that have developed in the status quo that can be remedied by Affirmative plan.

Impact—the part of a disadvantage scenario or Affirmative case that illustrates the terrible events that will occur if the other team's position is upheld. Impacts are caused by the other team's advocacy or by the absence of plan action.

Implementation specification (I-spec)—a theoretical argument made against the Affirmative team, accusing them of not adequately explaining how the plan would be implemented.

Inherency—the part of the 1AC outlining the barriers, such as a law or public opinion, in the status quo that prevent the Affirmative policy proposal from being passed.

Internal link—an optional part of a disadvantage or advantage that explains how the link will cause the impact.

Judge philosophy—a brief description of a judge's debating experience, preferred arguments, and preferred debate style.

Kritik—a Negative argument that claims the Affirmative's plan has a philosophical flaw.

Line by line—a form of debating in which arguments are presented in a numeric order following the same order as the previous speaker.

Link—the part of a disadvantage scenario showing how and why the Affirmative plan will cause an impact to occur.

Magnitude—the severity of an impact. Magnitude arguments are analytical and used to compare the impacts presented by the Affirmative and Negative teams.

Mutually exclusive—arguments and scenarios that call for two opposing actions and therefore cannot be supported simultaneously. Teams use the term "mutually exclusive" to notify the judge that she must choose only one argument to support at the end of the round.

Negative—the team assigned to oppose the Affirmative's proposal and/or the year's resolution.

Negative block—the 2NC and 1NR speeches, which occur with only a cross-examination period between them. Because the Affirmative does not speak between these speeches, they are often organized as if they were one long speech.

Net benefit—the argument used to differentiate between counterplan and plan solvency. The net benefit is either a disadvantage or solvency argument that applies to the Affirmative case but not the counterplan. The net benefit is used by the judge as a tiebreaker to determine who has won a plan/counterplan round.

Off-case—arguments presented by the Negative team that do not directly refute the evidence presented in the Affirmative case. Off-case arguments include counterplans, disadvantages, Kritiks, theory arguments, and topicality.

On-case—arguments that specifically attack the Affirmative's inherency, harms, advantages, or solvency.

Outweigh—a term indicating that one argument is more important than another.

Overview—a summary presented at the beginning of a rebuttal speech to highlight the most important arguments and provide a framework for evaluating all of the arguments in the debate round.

Permutation (perm)—a debate theory used by the Affirmative to argue that the plan and a counterplan or Kritik are not mutually exclusive. Permutations prove that both the Affirmative's and Negative's arguments could be adopted simultaneously.

Plan—the part of the 1AC case that advocates a specific policy initiative within the topic area. The Affirmative plan must be a declarative statement that endorses an action directly pertaining to the resolution.

Political disadvantage (politics)—a Negative argument claiming that the Affirmative plan will have dangerous repercussions on other polices being debated in Congress.

Pre-emption (pre-empt)—an argument made in anticipation of an argument in the opponent's next speech. Pre-emption arguments can be made early in the round and then extended or cross-applied in the rebuttal.

Preparation time (prep time)—the 10 minutes given to each team to gather their thoughts, organize their speeches, and ask the other team questions that they could not fit into cross-examination. Prep time may be used all at once or in small portions between speeches.

Prima facie—an argument that the judge must evaluate before all others. These arguments are often theoretical and challenge the opponent's conduct during the round.

Real world—a standard used in topicality, specification, and Kritik arguments to evaluate evidence and arguments on the basis of political, academic, or professional standards for deliberation.

Rebuttal—the last four speeches of a debate round. Rebuttal speeches must refute the opponent's arguments, build on the debaters' own critical arguments, and provide a compelling reason for the judge to award the debate round to the team.

Reason for Decision (RFD)—a judge's written or spoken testimony explaining how she evaluated the debate and why she voted for the winning team.

Refutation—arguments that disprove those of the opposing team.

Resolution—the predetermined policy proposal that is the topic of the debate.

Roadmap—a very brief statement before a speech that announces the order of a debater's arguments. The roadmap allows debaters and judges to organize their flows before the speech begins.

Scenario—a detailed story of how and why something will occur as a result of passing or failing to pass the Affirmative plan.

Shell—a preconstructed set of claims and warrants, including all necessary components of an argument. Shells are used by both the Affirmative and Negative teams to prepare and organize commonly used arguments and evidence.

Significance—a standard used in topicality and specification debates to evaluate the Affirmative plan. Significance asks if the

Affirmative plan is important enough to produce scholarship on both sides of the debate, thus allowing for a fair debate.

Solvency—part of the Affirmative case that explains how the plan will succeed in resolving the harms.

Specification—a type of theoretical argument claiming that the Affirmative has failed to specify the nuances of their plan, making the debate vague and unfair.

Speaker points—the individual points and ranking that a judge assigns to each debater at the end of the round. These points reflect the debater's presentation skill and argument quality. Speaker points are used as a tie-breaker after win/loss records to determine which teams will advance to elimination rounds.

Squad—the team of coaches and debaters from a college or university.

Status quo—a term used by debaters to describe to the current situation before the Affirmative plan is adopted.

Stock issues—the parts of the 1AC used to organize and present the desirability of the Affirmative plan. Affirmative teams are required to meet all five stock issues (inherency, harms, topicality, significance, and solvency) to win the round.

Tabula rasa—a theory used by the judge to evaluate arguments made during the round. Tabula rasa judges attempt to evaluate the round only on the arguments and evidence presented. Even if the judge is sure that evidence exists to contradict a position, she will not consider it unless it is presented by the debaters.

Tag—a concise statement that summarizes the thesis of a piece of evidence and states its significance in the debate.

Takeout—a defensive argument that refutes the opponent's claim.

Theory—a type of argument that challenges and defines the rules and norms of debate by claiming that the opposing team has violated those rules and norms.

Timeframe—the amount of time it will take for a scenario to occur.

Topic—a broad issue that is used to craft the year's resolution. The annual topic is determined by a process of democratic deliberation among debate squads.

Topicality—a Negative argument claiming that the Affirmative's case does not fall within the scope of the resolution. Topicality arguments claim that untopical Affirmative cases are unfair and should not win the round.

Turn—an offensive argument made by a debater to change the opponent's argument into one of her own.

Unconditional—a status of commitment where Affirmative and Negative teams choose to advocate their case, counterplan, or Kritik throughout the round without conditions.

Underview—a summary presented at the end of a rebuttal speech to highlight and evaluate the most important arguments and explain argumentative clashes that occurred during the round.

Uniqueness—information about the present state of affairs. Uniqueness evidence indicates that there is no risk of a scenario occurring in the status quo.

Voting issue (Voter)—an explicit reason why the opposing team should lose the debate based on a theory argument.

Warrant—the reason why a claim is justified. Warrants are presented either with evidence or analytical arguments.